# STREETWISE

## Homelessness Among the Young in Ireland and Abroad

D0258267

15 JUN 1998

By the same editor

*Who Should Care? The Development of Kilkenny Social Services.* Stanislaus Kennedy
RSC., Turoe Press, Dublin, 1981.

*One Million Poor? The Challenge of Irish Equality.* Ed. Stanislaus Kennedy RSC., Turoe
Press, Dublin, 1981.

*But Where Can I Go? Homeless Women in Dublin*, Stanislaus Kennedy RSC., Arlen
House, Dublin 1985.


Other Focus-Point productions

*Focus-Point Directory and Guide to Social Welfare, Health, Housing, Legal services and
other Social Services in Dublin.* Turoe Press, Dublin, 1985.

*Focus-Point Guide to Supplementary Welfare Allowance and Districts in Dublin, Wicklow
and Kildare. Who, Where, What and How of Supplementary Welfare Allowances*, Focus-
Point, Dublin, 1986.

*Nowhere To Go! The Challenge and Response to Homelessness in Ireland.* Focus-Point
Video Production, Dublin, 1986.

*Focus-Point in Focus.* Dublin, June 1987.


Focus-Point
14A Eustace Street
Dublin 2
Ireland

# STREETWISE

# Homelessness Among the Young in Ireland and Abroad

Edited by
Stanislaus Kennedy RSC

THE ECONOMIC & SOCIAL
RESEARCH INSTITUTE LIBRARY
15 JUN 1988
362·8

The Glendale Press

First published by The Glendale Press Ltd
18 Sharavogue
Glenageary Road Upper
Dun Laoghaire
Co. Dublin, Ireland

© Focus-Point and the contributors 1987


All rights reserved. No part of this publication may be reproduced, stored in a
retrieval system, or transmitted, in any form or by any means, electronic,
mechanical, photocopying, recording or otherwise, without the prior
permission in writing of the publisher.

ISBN 0 907606 52 0



Sponsored by Focus-Point, Dublin, UNICEF, New York, and Childhope, Guatemala.
1987 The International Year of Shelter for the Homeless




Cover design:  David L. Murphy
Photographs:  Rachel Collier
Design:  Duo Design
Text editor:  Siobhán Parkinson
Typesetting:  Wendy Commins, The Curragh, Co. Kildare.
Printing:  Kilkenny People Printing Ltd., High Street, Kilkenny.

# Contents

# Contributors

**Peter McVerry, SJ** is a member of the Society of Jesus and has lived and worked directly with the poor for thirteen years. He graduated from University College Dublin (MSc) and has spent six years working in Dublin's inner city and now lives and provides care and accommodation for young homeless people in Ballymun, Dublin. He is founder and director of the Arrupe Society for homeless boys and a member of the Jesuit Community's Centre for Faith and Justice. Following the Streetwise Conference in Dublin in 1987 he was appointed chairperson of the new national group, Streetwise.

**Stanislaus Kennedy** is a member of the Irish Sisters of Charity. She is a graduate of University College, Dublin (MSocSc) and of the University of Manchester (Diploma in Applied Social Studies). She was awarded an honorary doctorate in laws from Trinity College, Dublin in 1982. Sr Stanislaus is a Senior Research Fellow at UCD in the Department of Social Science. Currently a member of the Combat Poverty Agency and Co-ordinator of the Rural Projects of the EEC Programme to Combat Poverty, she is also founder and director of Focus-Point.

**Joseph Moerman** graduated in theology from the University of Louvain, Belgium. Between 1955 and 1965 he was appointed secretary general of Catholic education in Africa south of the Sahara. From 1967 to March 1985 he acted as secretary general of the International Catholic Child Bureau, and during this period (1977-1981) he became president of non-governmental organisations (NGO). Canon Moerman is a founding member and president of Defence for Children International (1980) and Childhope (1986). He is also president of the NGO Committee of UNICEF since August 1985.

**Victor Soler Sala** graduated in law from the University of Barcelona, Spain, and obtained a degree in development economics from Harvard University. He has worked for twenty-seven years with UNICEF, serving in various capacities both at the headquarters in New York and in regions of Latin America, south central Asia and south-east Asia. He worked as the UNICEF representative in Columbia and Indonesia, and served as regional director in the Middle East and north African Region. He was appointed to his present position in May 1986 as director of UNICEF in Geneva.

**Robert Hayes,** graduated from Georgetown University and New York University Law School. In 1985 he obtained the Martin Luther King Humanitarian Award. From 1982 to present, he has served as leader of and attorney to the National Advocacy Organisation

7

working for the rights of homeless people. He founded the organisation The National Coalition for the Homeless, opening a New York office in 1982 and a Washington Office in 1986, and has brought several major class action law suits which have established the right to shelter in New York city and the right of homeless people to vote.

**Steven Torkelsen** has worked for fifteen years for homeless children and their families in Canada, the United States of America and Central America. He obtained a master's degree in educational psychology and received a doctorate in social welfare in City University of New York Hunter College. He was Project Director of the first centre for streetchildren in New York — Covenant House. He helped establish Covenant House centres for street youth in Toronto and Heuston. He also worked for Covenant House in Guatemala city. Presently, Steven is senior vice-president of Covenant House and is based in New York. (Covenant House is one of the founding members of Childhope.)

**Nic Fenton**, a chartered accountant, was eleven years full-time director of the London hostel for homeless youth, Centrepoint. Since January 1987, he has been full-time deputy director of the Mental Health Association in the United Kingdom. In 1985 he became president of the European Young Homeless Group and in 1986 became a board member of Childhope. Nic is also currently a council member for the UK International Year of Shelter for the Homeless.

**Dr Joseph Robbins** is an Assistant Secretary in the Department of Health, Ireland, who has been responsible for services for various disadvantaged groups including the homeless and children in care. He holds a BA, B.Com.DPA and a PhD in Social History from Trinity College, Dublin. At the moment Dr Robbins is also Chairman of the Federation of Services for Unmarried Parents and their Children.

**Laetitia Lefroy** Senior Social Worker with Barnardo's since 1974, is Project Leader of the Social Work Services Project. She has extensive experience in fostering, adoption and residential care. For nine years Laetitia was responsible for Barnardo's work with HOPE, and she has retained a special interest in the problems of youth and homelessness.

**Marie Murphy RGS**, is a member of the Good Shepherd Sisters and has received a BA and HDip in education from University College, Cork, and a Diploma in Residential Child Care in Kilkenny. She has lectured in the principles and practice of child care in the Regional College, Waterford. She worked for twenty years in residential care in Ireland and spent three and a half years working with teenagers, in a residential setting in Tahiti. Since 1986 she has been a co-ordinator of the down-town services of the Good Shepherd Sisters for homeless women, children and young people in Cork.

**Derry O'Connor** was educated at University College, Dublin, where he graduated with a BSocSc degree. He has also completed an adult and community education diploma course in Maynooth College. Derry worked from 1972 to 1981 as a community-based youth worker in Dublin. He is currently assistant director of Comhairle Le Leas Óige Dublin.

8

**Majella Mulkeen** graduated from University College, Dublin, with a BSocSc in 1982. She received a diploma in community work in 1984 from St Patrick's College, Maynooth. She worked in residential care with teenage girls between 1984 and 1985 and has been working as an outreach worker in Focus-Point since 1985.

**Shane Sheridan** was educated in Dublin and worked in the architectural and building field before moving into youth work. He was involved in running a youth work experience project with National Manpower in Sandymount, Dublin, and for the following two years was a work experience officer in Scoil Ard Mhuire at Lusk. He graduated from University College, Cork as a professional social worker in 1985 (CQSW) after which he began work with Focus-Point as an outreach worker. In March 1987 Shane began work with the Eastern Health Board as a social worker with young homeless people.

**Shane Butler** graduated from University College, Dublin, with a BSocSc and has a master's degree in sociology. He has also completed a CQSW course in Manchester. Shane has worked as a social worker and as a researcher with the Eastern Health Board. He is currently a lecturer in social studies at Trinity College where he specialises in alcohol studies.

**Mervyn Ennis** trained as a youth and community worker in Moray House, Edinburgh and qualified in social work (CQSW) at Swansea University. He has worked as a youth worker for the Dublin Committee for Travelling People and he now works with the Eastern Health Board as a community worker in the south inner city of Dublin and also with Travelling people in Dublin.

**Margaret Maughan** was born in County Mayo and was one of seventeen children. She has been living for the past nine years in Dublin. Margaret attended school for five years and has been a participant in the Dublin Travellers' Education Resource at Beresford Place, Dublin, since 1985.

**John O'Brien** obtained a degree in social studies from Trinity College, Dublin. Since 1980 he has worked in Exchange House as a resource for Travelling people, in various capacities as youth worker, youth director and in his current position as director.

**Paula Scully** was educated at University College, Dublin, where she received a BcL degree. She qualified as a solicitor and has been a practising solicitor for the past ten years. Paula's special interest is children's law and she is currently working with the Legal Aid Board.

# Preface

When I was asked to chair the Streetwise conference which preceded this publication I felt like refusing. More papers, more discussion, more talk on the issue of young people out-of-home. People actively involved in the problem sharing yet again their frustrations at the lack of resources, the lack of planning, the apparent indifference of the decision-makers. *Action*, not *more discussion*, is what is needed.

But maybe, I felt, this could be the spur to action which is needed. Despite the failure of previous meetings to achieve much action, maybe this conference could be made to succeed.

The day itself was extremely useful. Much more important, however, a small group came together to ensure that some practical achievements would result from the conference. If this can happen then the conference was indeed worth while. This publication, I hope, will contribute to that process and so make the effort and contribution of all on that day a success.

In any developed country, the existence of young people forced to live on the streets is both a moral and a political scandal. Political indifference to the plight of young people, forced by circumstances to leave home, many of whom have already been scarred by their experience of neglect, violence and sexual abuse, is evidence of the moral decline of a nation.

Many of those working with young people out-of-home can testify to the abundant goodwill and concern of the ordinary people of Ireland. Their contributions and support have enabled many projects to continue and even expand in the face of diminishing statutory support. In this area, the people of Ireland are way ahead of our politicians. It is primarily they who stand indicted for the neglect of these young people for two reasons:

*Young Homelessness must be eliminated by political measures, not by charity.* Access to food, accommodation and the care and support that a young person's development requires is such a fundamental right that it cannot and should not be dependent on the goodwill of others. *The solution to*

11

*homelessness is not charity but justice*. Any civilised society must ensure that the basic needs of its children are guaranteed by the very structures of that society. Such a position goes beyond ideology whether of the right or of the left. Human compassion and decency demand it.

*Youth Homelessness is easily eliminated.*  The second reason why our politicians above all stand condemned by the continued existence of young people living on the streets is that this is a problem that can be *easily* eliminated. We could eliminate the problem almost overnight if we wished to. We are not dealing with a complex problem such as youth unemployment which is affected not only by decisions we make at home but also by international pressures and events over which we are relatively powerless. We are dealing with a problem which is completely within our ability here in Ireland to eliminate. It requires resources and effort. The history of the closure of Hope hostel and the subsequent opening of the hostel at Percy Place, recounted elsewhere in this publication, shows clearly that the effort is normally absent and the resources can be found when it is politically desirable.

Eliminating youth homelessness is simply not a political priority in Ireland. The politicians do not care enough about it. Hence the suffering of so many young people continues year after year, winter after winter.

There are, as always, broader issues involved. At this time no youth policy exists in this country despite the fact that almost 50 per cent of our population are under the age of twenty-five. Only within such a policy can the problems facing young people at risk, including young homeless people, be adequately faced, priorities assigned and the measures required to overcome the problems detailed. The absence of such a policy has contributed to the failure of the voluntary organisations dealing with young people out-of-home to co-ordinate their work. The services they provide have grown piecemeal and with little reference to existing services. Thus there exist both unnecessary duplication of services and huge gaps in services. This lack of co-ordination is primarily the responsibility of the voluntary organisations themselves. But it is difficult to co-ordinate services when the future of those services is so insecure. Most organisations dealing with young people out-of-home suffer from inadequate funding, little commitment from the statutory sector and no guarantees for the future. One organisation which had a three-year commitment from the coalition government found that its funding was abolished by the recent budget. Such a stop-go approach where decisions depend on short-term considerations or sometimes even the whim of the minister or prevailing political climate makes co-ordination of services almost impossible.

In Ireland, no single body has responsibility for young people out-of-home.

Responsibility is divided between the health boards, the Department of Justice, the Department of Education, the Department of Labour. Three hostels all providing a similar service to young people out-of-home are funded one by the Eastern Health Board, one by the Department of Justice and one by the Department of Education (out of the Sports Grant, no less!). Such division of responsibility ensures an inadequate provision of services.

Not only is it a scandal that this problem continues to exist — it is an absurdity. It is in society's own interest that we look after our young people. Young people do not become homeless because they are drug addicts or criminals or mentally disturbed. But they may become drug addicts, criminals or mentally disturbed by being homeless and neglected. Society will always pay the cost. And that same society will then turn round and *blame those young people whom they have neglected*!

One organisation with which I was involved approached a government department for £25,000 to open a hostel for a small number of young people who were homeless. Some young people had already been promised a place. While we were waiting for a response, one of these young people was sleeping in a bus and he lit a small fire to keep himself warm. Three buses went up in flames at a cost to the taxpayer of £250,000. It is more expensive *not* to provide for the needs of our young people.

Of course, expense is not the issue. Not only are we a sufficiently wealthy country to ensure that no young person need sleep rough but the right of a young person to accommodation, food and care is so basic that it ought to be amongst the highest priorities of any civilised society. A consensus on priorities is urgently needed today as cutbacks in public expenditure begin to bite. Every fundamental right that I can think of is being denied to some groups in society today and we have come to tolerate it. The right to food is denied to young people out-of-home under the age of eighteen who are not entitled to social welfare. Their choice is rob or starve, just as it was in the time of Dickens. The right to education is denied to many Travelling children by the failure to provide halting sites and the constant eviction of families from their unauthorised halts. The right to work is denied to 250,000 in our country. Even the right to life is already being denied to many by the failure to put adequate resources into the care and counselling of those diagnosed as AIDS antibody-positive. This failure is ensuring that many of them will spread the infection, imposing a death sentence on those they infect.

There are certain basic rights to which all are entitled and which must be protected at any cost. Yet we have a situation where these are denied to some, because, we are told, it costs too much, while others can get public assistance towards the purchase of luxury homes or get treatment at the Black-rock Clinic, while the political will to adequately tax certain groups or even collect what is due is absent.

If this publication can help to change our attitudes and policies towards young people out-of-home then it will have achieved its purpose.

Peter McVerry SJ

# Acknowledgements

To the authors for their willing response to my request for contributions to the seminar and to this book.

To UNICEF and Focus-Point staff for their help and support during the preparation of the seminar, especially to Dorothy Archer of UNICEF, Rachel Collier of Focus-Point and Peter McVerry SJ of the Centre for Faith and Justice.

To the many individuals, all of whom should be named and cannot be, but who know the share they have had in this book and where my gratitude lies.

To the publishers, The Glendale Press, for constant support during the preparation of the book.

Stanislaus Kennedy RSC

# Introduction

In March of this International Year of Shelter for the Homeless (1987) UNICEF and Focus-Point organised the seminar 'Streetwise' in Dublin, Ireland, to examine the situation of young people out-of-home and street-children both throughout the world and here in Ireland.

A group of people with a range of expertise and a variety of approaches in this area were invited to contribute, and this volume includes papers read at the seminar together with the findings and recommendations to come out of it. The seminar — and hence the book — had to be selective in what it dealt with, and the fact that certain issues are not dealt with here does not mean that we think they are unimportant. To supplement the papers actually read at the seminar, we include here also three extra papers, one on the UNICEF response to streetchildren throughout the world and two on the situation in the United States of America, as we felt that the issues raised in these papers complement those raised at the seminar.

### THE GLOBAL PERSPECTIVE
We don't know how many streetchildren exist in the world, but we do know that they are there and, as Canon Moerman puts it, 'one thing is certain: their number increases daily'. This statement is confirmed in the papers of Victor Soler Sala on the world situation and in particular on the situation in Latin America, Robert Hayes on the situation in the United States, Stephen Torkelsen on streetchildren in New York, and Nic Fenton on the situation in Europe.

Starved of love and care, streetchildren are victims not of war or natural disasters but of urban civilisation. The explosive growth of modern cities, the transition from extended to nuclear families, the extreme poverty, greed, affluence and the repressive attitudes of officialdom — any or all of these force these children out of their homes, out of institutions, very often onto the street, into a life of fear and exploitation.

### THE SITUATION IN IRELAND
If the present urbanisation trend continues the number of streetchildren will continue to grow, and this is happening here in Ireland, in Dublin and in our other cities, just as it has happened in other parts of the developed world.

17

The 'Streetwise' seminar took the global perspective into account, and it also focused, especially in the workshop sessions, on the situation in Ireland. As I pointed out in my own paper, there is a history of homelessness in this country that goes back to the eighteenth and nineteenth century and further, but the situation today, although of course partly caused by the economic circumstances in which we find ourselves, has grown up because of a variety of inadequacies, loop-holes and inconsistencies in our legislation and in our system of care and provision.

Although we don't have any firm statistics on the numbers of children and young people homeless and on the streets in this country, we at Focus-Point do have practical experience of hundreds of youngsters sleeping rough, squatting or dossing with friends and acquaintances, and we know that the hostel facilities that exist have been incapable at times over the past year of coping with the numbers that came to them. So even though we have no comprehensive research in Ireland on the extent of the problem, there can be no doubt that it is a growing phenomenon. As Peter McVerry says, the 'trickle of young people leaving home has now become a flood'.

In addition to the visible homeless, there are numbers of children who are homeless in effect, although they still physically live with their families. As Joe Robins puts it, 'A home means more than a roof over one's head; it also means love and acceptance and unity. Where these are absent there is no home.'

## INEQUALITY
Children who are out-of-home for whatever reason not only lose their home, which Marie Murphy describes as a basic human right, but 'this leads automatically', she goes on to point out, 'to the loss of equality and opportunity in almost every sphere of social living'. And this inequality is reflected in the papers of Shane Sheridan and Majella Mulkeen of Focus-Point's Outreach team, of Mervyn Ennis and Margaret Maughan who focus on the plight of the Travelling community, of Shane Butler who highlights the neglect of the problems of drug abuse, and of John O'Brien who describes the work of Exchange House in providing services for Travelling children and their families. families.

## POOR PROVISION
Over and over again the seminar was reminded of the situation of young people over twelve years of age who cannot stay at home. Although services for younger children and babies have improved in recent years, it has been at the expense of the older child, and it is virtually impossible to place a child over twelve in residential care; the situation is even more difficult for the over-

fourteens. Added to this are inadequate therapeutic care, emergency accommodation, day activity centres, child-guidance services, assessment centres and support and services for families.

Difficult as it is to find places for younger teenagers, the situation of young adults in the sixteen-to-eighteen age group is many times worse. These young people are too old for care and too young for social welfare payments as adult members of society — they fall well and truly into a no-man's-land of provision. The state is under no legal obligation either to support them or to provide them with housing.

These anomalies in provision are due to a fragmented and piecemeal approach to services. Derry O'Connor points out in his paper the lack of a comprehensive youth policy and service. As long as we continue to make inadequate provision in this uncoordinated fashion, young people will, as Laetitia Lefroy says in her paper on residential care, 'continue to become streetwise'. Our lack of a properly co-ordinated policy and framework means that we simply pass responsibility around from one body to the next, with the voluntary sector stretched to its limits in the effort to fill in the gaps left by inadequate statutory provision.

The reality is that our statutory children's services, under the Department of Health and the health boards, are unable to cater for our youngsters who cannot stay at home. Because of this situation, these children and young adults become both actually homeless and stigmatised with the label of homelessness. This label carries many connotations: dirty, lazy, no-good, alcoholic, delinquent, drug addict. And because these children, largely through no fault of their own, are labelled differently, they tend to be perceived differently. How we perceive people affects our attitudes to them, and our attitude to these out-of-home youngsters is that they are difficult, they are turbulent, they are problematic, they are troublesome, they are undeserving. So we provide *separate* services for them in *separate* hostels or houses, and what services there are are provided not by the statutory bodies but by underfunded voluntary agencies. This in turn reinforces society's attitudes towards these children, that they don't deserve any better.

Inadequate provision is compounded by outmoded and unhelpful legislation: Paula Scully points out that homeless people are lumped together in law with common criminals, persons up for indecent exposure and persons charged with having offensive weapons, among others. Again, the way in which we perceive homeless people affects the way in which we provide for them — or fail to provide for them.

19

## THE EXPERIENCE OF HOMELESSNESS FOR YOUNGSTERS

For many of these youngsters, the street or the squat often replaces school and has a very different syllabus. In a sense, the places they inhabit belong to nobody and to everybody; everyone is on the same footing.

These children's lives are unstructured and destabilised. When they awake in the morning these young people cannot be sure where the next meal is coming from, or indeed if there will be one. They have to take everything, however ghastly, in their stride. They cannot make any plans. They are like weather-cocks, playthings of circumstances, at the mercy of the first suggestion made, and sometimes they scarcely seem to know whether they are coming or going.

Some of these children may have been in institutions, in very structured settings, but in a very short time after leaving the institutions they can lead such unstructured lives that all structure can move away from them, not necessarily because they deliberately reject structure, but because they simply have no structures to conform to.

In the long run, this sense that nothing is stable can produce distortions of the mind. Many young people on the streets lose track of time and do not know for how long they have been wandering around with no structure or specific purpose. They are unable to describe clearly their activity on a given day. Distance too may be a vague concept.

These children perceive the streets and the squats differently from the rest of us, for them these places can be productive or barren, friendly or un-friendly, at different times of the day or night. Sometimes places outside their immediate experience are simply unknown territory to them. Others move quite a lot, and moving about, whether from area to area or just within a limited area, makes it difficult for them to form lasting human relation-ships. Consequently, many are emotionally immature and they desperately need the affection and the presence of mature adults.

In this anonymous world physical danger is all too real. Visibility means not protection but vulnerability. The possibility of violence is ever present. These youngsters know the fear of brutality at the hands of others. They also know the fear of disease, the fear of the police, the fear of being put away. They must give as good as they get, and may even terrorise passers-by. To these youngsters, violence is part of the language of deprivation and perhaps no more than a logical consequence of the violence of which they have been victims in their own families and later outside the family. This violence is often misunderstood by society and we respond to the symptom rather than the cause.

20

Harsh though their life is, it would be wrong to think that for them their life is always miserable. On the contrary, visitors to shanty towns are often surprised by the apparent cheerfulness and generosity of the inhabitants; similarly, young people out-of-home, who have known systematic neglect or rough treatment at home, seem to make light of their afflictions and turn a bright face on the world, at least for a short time. Even those who live entirely alone can think of it as one step up from their previous suffering within their family. With this dizzying lifestyle, the thrills, pills and variety, their lives can exert an undeniable fascination for a while, and some need contact and strong trusting relationships before they try any alternative which can be offered them.

Life with a group can provide protection, comradeship, a substitute family, status and excitement, rules to which, unlike those of the conventional society, the young person can conform. In particular, it also meets the need for a sense of identity for these young people.

In normal family life the shock of adolescence is cushioned, allowing the youngster a gradual emergence into society. When this is lacking, youngsters cannot get their bearings and are vulnerable to the first influence they meet outside. The teenage years bring their own emotional and social problems, including a harder attitude on the part of the public. That is why young people need protection, especially young people between twelve and eighteen years. When that protection cannot be given in the home it must be given by child-care statutory authorities. Otherwise young people are exposed to a situation that makes them very vulnerable indeed. With help, this vulnerable group may grow towards some kind of solution of its predicament. Otherwise they will tend to remain misfits in one way or another.

## CONCLUSION

There are no justifiable reasons for youth homelessness. Governments may argue that there are no funds to make adequate provision for young people, but it is not a question of funds or resources — it is a question of priorities and values. Unfortunately, decisions relating to children's services are very often based on political expediency rather than on social need. Loughan House was turned into a secure unit for young people who had broken the law almost overnight in 1978, and the same situation emerged again in 1984 when Spike Island was turned into a prison for young people. Yet it took nine months to replace Hope hostel, the only short-term hostel in Dublin for young homeless boys. It seems that the lobbies who are concerned about the protection of property have more clout than those of us who are concerned about the protection and safety of young people.

The voluntary agencies face a dilemma: as long as they continue to provide services for young people with inadequate funding, so long can they in a sense be said to be colluding with the system that pushes these young people out to the periphery. The voluntary bodies must see to it that statutory bodies carry out their responsibility to ensure that these young people are given the sort of care that they need and that is appropriate for them. At present these young people have fallen between the cracks and have come to be labelled as homeless simply because there is no provision for them.

When life becomes unbearable for children they fade. They do not necessarily fall ill and die, but they fade in other ways. They create chaos, throw tantrums, provoke disharmony, divide their families, become loners, fail at school, they truant, they steal, they lie, they dabble in alcohol and drugs, and finally they run away from home. This is a process that could be arrested for many at an early stage, if the services were available to them.

Many of us tend to believe that there is a growing problem of youth homelessness in New York, Guatemala, London, Cairo, Paris and other large cities but fail to recognise the problem in our own country. One of the greatest challenges facing us in Ireland today is to face up to the fact that *we* have a growing problem of youth homelessness and streetchildren in our cities who are being exploited socially, emotionally, physically and sexually, and we as a society are not responding. If we continue to turn a blind eye to the problem the situation is likely to grow to the same proportions as it has grown to in other cities which are described in this book.

Youth homelessness is something that shouldn't exist; this is a book that should not need to be written. Youth homelessness is not something we can blame on God, or on other people: the blame lies squarely with all of us as a society, with our administrators, and with you and me. It is we who, in this last quarter of the rich twentieth century, have unthinkingly, recklessly and readily created and supported that which is intolerable for many of our children and young people. There is still time to turn our callousness and indifference into a call for justice and concern.

Stanislaus Kennedy RSC

THE
GLOBAL
PERSPECTIVE

# Streetchildren and the International Year of Shelter for the Homeless

I was very happy to learn some years ago that an International Year of Shelter for the Homeless (IYSH) was being planned. I felt that this could be the most 'child-minded' year since the International Year of the Child (1979), since shelter, by its very nature, is a family problem, and therefore a child problem too. Streetchildren are one of the most preoccupying child problems today, and shelter must be a priority for those concerned with streetchildren.

## SHELTER FOR THE HOMELESS IN DEVELOPING AND INDUSTRIALISED COUNTRIES

There is a tendency among people of industrialised countries not to be interested in the activities of the United Nations. Industrialised countries see the UN as being concerned only with the developing countries, the so-called Third World, and richer countries tend to be self-interested and unconcerned about problems and solutions that they see as unrelated to them.

This attitude on the part of the wealthier countries is part of the reason for the financial and indeed moral crisis that now faces the UN: some financially strong countries feel uncommitted to the UN because they feel that their own country does not benefit from its activities. Needless to say, this is ethically unacceptable, but it is also factually inaccurate: certainly funds go to the developing countries, but the UN is concerned also with the problems of the countries of the northern hemisphere — whether these problems are of a scientific, economic, social, demographic or other nature — and the difference in approach is simply that the industrialised countries do not receive financial assistance, but are expected to raise funds from their own resources to solve their problems.

There is no excuse for such indifference when it comes to the problem of shelter for the homeless, for this is a problem common to industrialised and developing countries, as a walk across practically any city in the northern hemisphere will show. We have slums in most industrialised cities as poor as those in most Third World countries. In industrialised countries too, there are many families who do have homes, but who are paying such high rents that they have very little income left for other basic necessities. Where we are poor or how we become poor does not matter, but when the source of poverty is an outrageously high rent, then those committed to the ideals of IYSH cannot remain passive.

Shelter for the homeless is a challenge to all of us, because of the problems of homelessness in the developing countries, and because of the problems of housing in the industrialised countries. We should all support the UN initiative and the IYSH.

### FAMILIES AND CHILDREN
Those who should benefit most from this year of action on homelessness and who should be the most direct target of this year are families and children. I see this year as being a family/child year in particular. Everybody needs shelter, from the strongest athlete, the soldier in war and the astronaut to the nomad, the vagrant, the so-called unsettled or travelling population, we all need a safe place to rest, eat, sleep, be protected from the weather, but a family needs more than a roof over its head, and has a more urgent reason to need it: a family needs a home. A home is called a *foyer* in French, which literally means a fireplace; it is a word that evokes warmth and love. How can a family play its social role as a loving and caring institution, an educational unit, a secure environment for the children without a shelter that is really what we call home?

It is people who create a home: many luxurious shelters are unfortunately not real homes, because they lack a loving atmosphere. On the other hand, it is difficult to create the desired atmosphere of a home without the material conditions for accommodation. All this is quite obvious, but I want to make one important point here: if it is true that a shelter should become a real home for all the members of the family, it is also true that when there is failure to establish a home, it is the children who are the principal victims, because they are the most vulnerable. They miss care, love and security; their education is interrupted; they have to live most of the time outside of the family context, and if things come to the worst, they become streetchildren.

It is because of our love and concern for children that I encourage members of child-related organisations and projects to support the action of International Year of Shelter for the Homeless at national and international level. We need to urge the authorities, national and international, to take concrete and effective measures to provide every family with at least a decent place to live, in love and harmony.

### STREETCHILDREN
I see the International Year for Shelter for the Homeless as a year of special

importance for children on the street. The phenomenon of streetchildren has always existed in some countries: it was for instance a serious problem in the early days of industrialisation in England at the beginning of the last century. In some countries it has disappeared following adequate social action; in other countries, for instance in the new urban areas of several developing countries, it has recently appeared; and in others again it has reappeared, as in many industrialised countries today. But the magnitude and worldwide character of the problem were only revealed in the International Year of the Child. Up to then there existed projects and programmes operating with or without public support, but working largely in isolation.

The numbers of streetchildren have never been exactly known, and worldwide figures vary from 30 to 80 million. But one thing is certain: their numbers are increasing daily.

Streetchildren can be roughly grouped into two categories: runaways, children who have broken with their families; and children who remain part of the family unit, but who are sent into the streets by their families to beg, thieve or traffic. Then there are children who live partly on the street, but who are loosely attached to their families, and there are children who are still with their families but who are at risk and who, unless their conditions are rapidly improved with help from outside, will soon join the streetchildren.

These children are all in one way or another victims of failure of the family, whether they leave home or whether they are pushed out of the home: there is not much difference between running away if you are maltreated, starved or made to feel unwanted and being pushed out onto the street. And in many cases the families of these children are themselves unstable: there may be a single parent, or a mother and a man who is not the children's father and who maltreats children who are not his own, or indeed a conventional two-parent family where violence between the parents is the norm.

In any case, the problem of streetchildren is worsening daily. In countries where the problem did not exist at all, for instance in sub-Saharan Africa, it is becoming a fast-growing process, parallel to the increasing industrialisation and urbanisation. Bad accommodation and homelessness are themselves a major cause of other problems: break-up of families, poor health and nutrition and recourse to the street by children as their normal and habitual abode.

## ACTION ON STREETCHILDREN
Public awareness began to focus on the problem of streetchildren as a direct effect of the International Year of the Child, and action began to be taken.

In 1982 the International Catholic Child Bureau, of which I was at that time secretary general, decided to set up a three-year programme, involving various non-government organisations (NGOs), to identify already existing activities, to evaluate them, to create links among their pioneers, to promote the establishment of new programmes and to bring the problem to the attention of public opinion and policy-makers. In co-operation with Pauline Berwick, who was in charge of the (Catholic) Council for Social Welfare, I convened a dozen local street-workers in Dublin, several of whom did not know each other and were surprised to hear of other action groups than their own.

Parallel to this development among the NGOs, UNICEF also increased its involvement in work on behalf of streetchildren from 1982 onwards. Its regional programme on behalf of abandoned and streetchildren in Latin America and the Caribbean was spectacularly successful. UNICEF's alternative, preventative, community-based approach was quite revolutionary for this kind of work and the agency was (and is) crucial in bringing governments and NGOs together in pioneering pilot projects in areas where there is little experience, and in advocating in general on behalf of these children. These programmes have recently been extended to such countries as Ethiopia, Kenya, Somalia, Sudan, the Philippines and Thailand.

**CHILDHOPE**
By the end of August 1985, when the inter-NGO programme had come to an end, it had to be decided whether the work should be put on a more permanent basis. I had become increasingly aware of the necessity for a real network at national and international level, to co-ordinate the work of existing programmes and to facilitate contacts among the workers involved. Since there was no existing NGO that felt capable of assuming this heavy burden, a new *ad hoc* organisation was established in April 1986: Childhope — a movement on behalf of streetchildren.

With an operational base in Guatemala, its activities will embrace all continents. This new organisation, although non-governmental, is strongly supported by UNICEF in the frame of the follow-up of the very important resolution adopted by its executive board in 1986 on 'children in especially difficult circumstances'. This is a new and very impressive example of how initiatives originated in non-governmental circles can lead to joint action by UNICEF and NGOs. (See also the paper in this book by Victor Soler Sala.)

**INTERNATIONAL YEAR OF SHELTER FOR THE HOMELESS**
Unlike other international years, International Year of Shelter for the Homeless has an objective that can easily be translated into concrete action. It stems from real and perceivable needs, and can lead to workable proposals

for solution. Extended housing policies will have to be launched in developing countries, and policies for accessible housing rates will have to be reinforced in industrialised countries. Moreover, we do not have to start from scratch. There are already many examples of cheap and decent housing all over the world. Many of these schemes have been initiated by missionaries or other people belonging to Christian development agencies.

However, a full and satisfactory solution to the problem will not be reached on the basis of technical improvements only. For this question as for many others, the heart of the problem is a problem of the heart. It is not only a technological but also a behavioural problem. The public at large in our industrialised countries should agree that the hundreds of millions of homeless people in developing countries and the dozens of millions in industrialised countries are a shame on humankind and a challenge to each of us.

Even from a selfish point of view, we should realise that the problem of the growing number of children on the streets is not only a tragedy for the children but a threat to established society. Obliged to live on the profits of theft or illicit trafficking, exploited sexually or through drugs, these children will not passively accept spending their adulthood in misery, homelessness and economic slavery. When thousands of marginalised youngsters grow up, the cities are in danger of becoming unmanageable.

To tackle this problem we need to build up attitudes and habits that result in a better sharing of living space and comfort among all human beings and actively support all initiatives in this field. We all have something to do. If we agree, in our daily lives, in our everyday environment and through the structures and organisations at our disposal, to tackle this reality to the best of our ability, we can create a world movement to provide shelter for those who need it and thus contribute to the solution of the staggering situation of homeless children, the millions of streetchildren. If you think of streetchildren and if you have a compassionate heart, you will not hesitate to be inventive and to contribute solutions. In this way, International Year of Shelter for the Homeless can be a real 'childhope' year.

by Canon J. Moerman

Childhope may be contacted at the following addresses:
Childhope, PO Box 20423, Dag Hammareskjold Center, New York, NY 10017
Childhope/Esperanza de los Niños, Apartado Postal 992-A, Cuidad Guatemala, Guatemala CA

# Streetchildren: A Major Concern for the Coming Years

**INTRODUCTION AND OVERVIEW**

The large numbers of abandoned and streetchildren in both developing and industrialised countries today represent a serious social challenge to us all. While the quiet presence of many of these youngsters is unobtrusive and often ignored, the dramatic sight of a smaller number who roam city centres in bands or gangs evokes alarm amongst citizens and the media. Day centres and full-time institutions have become over-crowded, and boys and girls who lack adequate family support have been left to drift, or have been actually cast off to survive alone at what appears to be an increasingly young age. Collectively these forgotten children represent a tragic loss to this generation and an ever more severe handicap for the next. Some have estimated that these children of want may number as many as 80 million in our world today, of whom approximately half live in Latin America.

The severe economic crisis, debt and structural adjustment now affecting many developing countries have not only led to internal financial and emotional strains upon families, but have, in a very real sense, robbed children of their childhood, forcing them into city streets, marketplaces and factories to earn what little they can to try to ensure their families' very survival. The increasing separation of family members, coupled with the added vulnerability of the child on the street, places each of these young people at very high risk of eventual family loss and abandonment. Girls, who are increasingly evident amongst streetchildren, are particularly vulnerable in such situations — more disenfranchised (often by far) than their brothers, and certainly more susceptible to physical and sexual exploitation.

Particularly in Latin America and Asia, an increasing tide of rural-to-urban migration has sent millions of families scurrying to the metropolis in search of a share in the new city prosperity. The urban populations of Brazil, Colombia and Mexico have increased by from 30 to 70 per cent since 1945. In that same period, the population of Manila has grown five times, and Bangkok has increased in size by seven. Large city slums such as Nairobi's 'Mathere Valley' (pop. 120,000) and Rio de Janeiro's 'Rocinha' (pop. 130,000) have become as cities unto themselves, but with few of the basic services and little of the human cohesion which new residents from the countryside dreamed of as the urban gift. Indeed, great cities such as Mexico, where approximately 1500 rural immigrants put down new roots daily, find their capacity to serve new residents taxed well beyond the limits.

## WHO ARE THE STREETCHILDREN?

Despite the hardships which daily assault families in poor urban communities of developing countries, the majority of children have homes and enjoy adequate, consistent family support relative to the community's reality. These 'home children' may account for as many as 75 per cent of the child population, and may include also youngsters with less secure family support, but who are still too young to be working outside the home, as well as children whose families are at such high risk that they become the most logical candidates for the street if no remedial action is taken.

Not all children, however, are as fortunate. A large number whose family support base has become increasingly weakened must share in the responsibility for family survival by working on city streets and marketplaces. For these children on the street, the home ceases to be their centre for play, culture and daily life. Nevertheless, while the street becomes their daytime activity, most of these children will return home most nights. While their family relationships may be deteriorating, they are still definitely in place, and these children continue to view life from the point of view of their families. They still strongly belong to their parent(s) and siblings. Accounting for as many as half of a given community's child population, these young people can easily be spotted (usually outside of their own neighbourhoods and in city centres) selling shopping bags, candy, chewing gum or cigarettes, shining shoes, or caring for automobiles. Often they are involved in more than one type of sale or service to make ends meet; sometimes their work is seasonal or related to special days of the week or year. The work they must perform to support their family's and their own survival is not always what we would term lawful and morally appropriate. A number become involved in petty thievery, pickpocketing, drug trafficking, prostitution, pornography. Many children in this grouping, made increasingly vulnerable to abuse and exploitation in street life, come to have an increasingly weakened self-esteem and an increasingly negative view of themselves.

Finally, most but not all communities have a much smaller number of children who daily struggle for survival without family support, alone. These youngsters become children of the street, whose ties with home have now been broken and who, *de facto*, are without families. This group also includes of course orphans, institutionalised children, runaways, and young people who have become refugees, displaced, soldiers, bonded apprentices, and slaves. Whether

31

declared abandoned or not, abandonment is deeply felt by the child. What is often interpreted as the 'irregular behaviour' of these children is really an adjustment to the blow of being alone in life. Fortunately, this hardest hit group of youngsters is usually very small in number, accounting for perhaps no more than 5 per cent of the total child population of a community, city or country.

## APPROACHES TO IMPROVING THE LIVES OF STREETCHILDREN

UNICEF is concerned with the protection of all 'children in especially difficult circumstances' in general and of streetchildren in particular. At its 1986 session, UNICEF's executive board had before it a policy review paper on children in especially difficult circumstances and a series of supporting documents.

Exploitation may to some extent be prevented or diminished by the adoption of new legislation or the enforcement of existing legislation with regard to children at work and children on the street. Protection and support are needed, especially for younger children because of their greater vulnerability, and the greater urgency for meeting their support and development needs.

A second approach to improving the lives of working children and streetchildren is to provide them with basic services such as health care, nutrition and education, both through services that are made available to the community as a whole and through special activities directed specifically to them.

The success of such innovative approaches can be measured in terms of meeting their objectives of building individual lives, building and restoring families, and developing strong active communities. Perhaps no other criterion is so important as the well-being of each child. To what extent are his or her physical and psycho-social needs being met? Does he or she feel happy and satisfied with life? Do the projects and programmes assist the children to meet their needs of income generation, education and vocational preparation? The needs of the entire family (if there still is one) and the restoring of it to collective good health with a secure future are also important. Prevention of further family separation and disintegration for children who have families, as well as the re-incorporation of homeless children into new families, can also be real marks of an initiative's success. While numbers of children reached are frequently used to judge social impact of such projects, qualitative evaluation of life impact is just as important. Very often in such assessments, the children and their parents can be the very best judges of how valuable an undertaking on their behalf has been. Such face-to-face information collection may not be scientific, but it frequently provides the best answers to our questions.

## WORKING WITH CHILDREN AT HOME

In many poor urban communities, large numbers of children face the unhappy realities of increasing separation within their natural families. Home relationships may deteriorate to the point of the child's abandoning his or her family or becoming abandoned by it. So children at home are also a group at risk. Experience tends to indicate that the most successful approach may be the expansion of more and better basic services to poor communities. The provision of such services combats family disintegration by improving the quality of family life. The introduction of a few such services frequently leads to the provision of others, and to an extended service coverage. Often, a community coming together to discuss specific needs will also come to examine other broader concerns such as streetchildren. Such micro-planning by communities can become strong deterrents to family separation and child abandonment — especially when family counselling becomes a programme component.

## WORKING WITH CHILDREN ON THE STREET

Once out of the house, usually at seven or eight years of age, children face both the increased risks of family separation and the increased dangers of the street itself.

An important consideration in working with these children is that they are still part of families and communities, even though greater separation may be on the horizon. In the past, many private and governmental projects on behalf of streetchildren have considered these children on the street to be really of the street or even abandoned, and placed them in closed institutional programmes, which further isolated them from their families and communities. Sometimes they were even offered for adoption before it was confirmed that they were really without family support. Often the most severe difficulties of the families of these children are temporary (such as illness) or can be resolved by the provision of family support mechanisms. Working with the families of these children provides us also with a chance to work with the communities of which they are a part, benefiting an entire neighbourhood instead of just one child removed from it. In Brazil in 1983, a comparative cost analysis of closed and open projects on behalf of streetchildren indicated that such community approaches were from five to ten times less expensive than traditional institutions.

It is towards the children on the street that UNICEF's recent efforts (particularly in Latin America) have been directed. While not yet *of* the street and still of the family, they are most often found *on* the street — and are often at very high risk of losing their homes. UNICEF's regional programme on behalf of abandoned and streetchildren in Latin America has emphasised the provision of urban basic services in these youngsters' communities as well as special child services to them on the street where they work and spend most of their waking hours. Frequently the local initiatives which are encompassed by this regional programme have used urban basic services as an entry point into the community, and encouraged parallel street-oriented projects providing for the needs of working children who are not in the community during the day.

The undertakings which have had the most impact upon the lives of these children on the street have always faced up to the two principal needs of these young people: income generation as a protected dignifying experience, and education appropriately adapted to the child today and to his or her adult needs tomorrow. In fact, many enlightened project leaders have seen work and education as a single process — complementary to the reality of today and hopeful of a better reality tomorrow — inappropriate and ineffectual if separated. Very often, given the cruelly exploitative situation in which many streetchildren find themselves, there is the need both for alternative education and alternative work — a protective net that will allow sound child development to take place, including the restoration of a major part of childhood.

To be sure, income generation and alternative education are not the sole considerations of successful projects for these children, but they are the first ones. Recreation and play have often been seen not just as relaxation for the children but also as an integral part of the work-and-learning process. Nutrition, health and dental services and socio-psychological support have also played important roles for all members of the children's families. Most effectively, all of these project components have been brought together as an integral process which brings boys and girls who have formerly seen themselves as unworthy, a new self-esteem, self-confidence, and self-direction — giving quality to new lives by building on the best of former ones.

It is worth mentioning at this point the singularly important role played by street educators in successful local initiatives on behalf of streetchildren. For reasons emanating from street and home alike, many of these youngsters have experienced a draining away of confidence in all adults. Because of constant abuse and exploitation, it is impossible for some to believe that an approaching man or woman has anything but an ulterior motive in mind, or that an adult would offer a streetchild something without wanting as much or much more in return. Acceptance by these young people of people who are older and bigger is understandably very difficult indeed. For this reason, initial contacts, the offering of friendship, and the building of acceptance and confidence cannot be accomplished by just any adult.

The street educator, very often a former streetchild himself or herself, is a uniquely important person in establishing and developing child-to-adult-to-child relationships in this context. He or she goes to where the child is on the street, works around the clock according to the streetchild's accustomed routine, offers comfort, understanding and protection (often at great personal risk). Offering respect rather than eager paternalism, the street educator is able to gradually gain the trust of the streetchildren, and help them to direct their lives into a programme in which they share the design and development — focusing upon the two major elements mentioned previously: income generation and alternative education.

THE ROLE OF INSTITUTIONS

There has been a very long history of traditional responses to the problems of children of the street and abandoned children, many of which are very discouraging. The unhappy results of formal and informal adoptions and the long lingering years spent by many youngsters in large unfriendly (even brutal) institutions have been widely written about over many generations.

Clearly, serious attention must be paid to these boys and girls. If there must be institutions for such youngsters, let them be as humane and personable as possible with family groupings (such as those in Pueblito in Costa Rica) and, where possible, they should be just a transitional step towards obtaining new permanent families (as in the case of the Chavilito programme in Nicaragua). And, where the child has been clearly abandoned or orphaned, let the declaration of that abandonment be executed as expeditiously as possible to allow the child a new family by adoption before he or she passes an entire childhood in an institution.

ALTERNATIVE FAMILIES

It is of the utmost importance that children who still have families (as in the case of many children of the street as well as refugee, displaced and migrant children) should not be considered abandoned simply because a parent is not to be seen or found immediately. The International Red Cross has been extremely meticulous in such situations, especially during emergencies.

The most successful local experiences in working with the children of the street have always made the best situation possible under existing local circumstances. When adoption and fostering have been possible, they have been carefully and effectively promoted. When these options have not been possible (usually for cultural reasons) family-like groupings have been arranged such as group homes within a regular community or caretaker families within children's villages. Nevertheless there is still much creative thinking to be done with regard to possible 'new families', for children of the

35

street particularly. For example, it was the street children themselves who, in Sao Paulo, organised themselves into a new family and sought out a favoured street educator to be their house parent. Such arrangements may not conform to local interpretations of what is a nuclear family unit, but they do often provide the essential support and protection which a family can offer as well as its most essential contributions to the child: someone who really cares personally and a personal identity for each young person.

The consequences of not seeking families for these children — committing them to an anonymous childhood in massive institutions, or letting them rear themselves on the city streets, or permitting them a childhood and adolescence of servitude in the homes of better-off families — can be disastrous for the child now and for the child's children in the future. Clearly the most effective long-term response would be to prevent children from coming this far along the separation continuum, that is to prevent them losing their families in the first place. However, the reality is that today in our world there are at least several million of these youngsters. Given each country's available resources, human and economic, a substantial resolution to these children's problems should be possible within the next few years.

### A NEW HOPE FOR TOMORROW
Recent experiences such as those referred to above have shown beyond doubt that there is reason for hope and optimism. The sheer numbers of street-children and the amount of suffering they represent have much too often made people close their eyes and turn their backs to the problem. Yet there *is* hope of seeing real change on behalf of these children within our lifetime. Latin America is showing the way. In countries like Brazil, Colombia, and Mexico, a wave of empathy, understanding, and determination amongst the government, state agencies for child and family welfare, social workers, the churches, voluntary organisations, universities, and beyond is resulting in programmes that are gradually turning into people's movements.

UNICEF's own experience confirms such hopes.

Perhaps the most effective role which UNICEF has played to date has been that of an advocate on behalf of abandoned and streetchildren — as an agent for changing attitudes and ideas. The Brazil model serves as the best example. Through the identification and systematisation of five existing community projects in 1982, the UNICEF government team was able to show that there really were alternatives to institutionalising streetchildren or to not taking any action at all. Through documenting these successful experiences and sharing their principles and techniques with representatives of other communities in workshops, seminars and exchange visits, and by working closely

36

with the church and key non-government organisations, the Brazil national project became increasingly more effective in extending hope and initiating further community action, to the point where today the team is working with some 400 local groups throughout the country. The Brazilian government, through its central child agency, the National Foundation for Child Welfare (FUNABEM), has incorporated this community-oriented preventative approach of working with the children on the street into its operating policies, and has even applied the National Street Child Project's methodology in working with children in other areas within its programme mandate.

Regionally, in Latin America, inter-country exchange visits, communications networking, and regional seminars have achieved strong beginnings for a Latin American movement on behalf of abandoned and streetchildren. This programme has also had an important impact inter-regionally and internally within UNICEF, providing technical assistance to such African countries as Kenya and Mozambique as well as to the Philippines and Thailand in Asia.

Linked closely to advocacy has been the technical assistance role of UNICEF. In Brazil, Colombia and Mexico, for example, UNICEF has worked closely with the national, state and local government authorities in the development of more effective alternative community models for working with streetchildren.

In Latin America particularly, UNICEF has become increasingly effective in the dissemination of project-building information and materials, as well as in the development of human resources and resource networks -- principally through its support of field-training practicums and local-national workshops.

UNICEF has also been instrumental in the development of special techniques to facilitate local initiatives. Situation analysis of streetchildren became particularly effective as a starting point for projects in the Philippines, and in determining appropriate places to begin department-wide streetchild actions in Colombia. Micro-planning as a tool has proved particularly effective in designing local streetchild projects in Bucaramanga, Columbia and Cuatzacualcos, Mexico and monitoring and evaluation techniques have made a substantial contribution to the development of the national project in Brazil.

Much remains to be done. That goes without saying. Successful programme experiences from Latin America need to be extended to Africa and Asia on a broader scale than now, even if the lessons of the Americas' region have already been shared with Mozambique, Kenya, Ethiopia, Somalia, the Philippines and Thailand resulting in new and innovative projects.
Awareness, concern and commitment need to be better mobilised in developing and industrial countries alike.

Serious research is desperately needed, particularly in the form of practical, action-oriented studies and assessments of concerns directly affecting the daily lives of streetchildren, such as the means of protecting streetchildren at work, income generation with dignity, training effectively for adult employment, the role of the street educator, literacy training and alternative schooling for streetchildren, family and community involvement, needs of and activities for streetgirls, and how to begin a streetchild project.

Local projects --- often isolated — need to be brought together and matched with international resources, both human and material.

The list of what needs to be done could be extended infinitely. But just as important these needs are gradually but increasingly being met.

1987 and beyond will be years that will see UNICEF's Childhope, governments and local groups and organisations join hands in effective action for streetchildren. The work is under way. There *is* hope!

by Victor Soler Sala

# Homelessness in the United States

Homelessness has reached epidemic proportions in the United States, with upwards of three million Americans without a place to live. Traditionally it took a national depression or economic panic to trigger mass homelessness. Today, Wall Street enjoys record profits, while record numbers of the dispossessed cram into barbaric municipal shelters a mile north of Wall Street.

As with poverty across the United States, homelessness — that most grievous symptom of poverty — is afflicting the young most viciously. The public perception of the homeless (either an alcoholic, elderly man typically of Irish descent or a mentally disturbed, middle-aged woman) has not kept pace with the reality of the streets.

Increasingly across the United States, the majority of homeless persons are children. Tonight in New York City there will be more homeless children living in that city's massive, emergency shelter system than the total number of homeless single men and women combined. That fact should not be surprising: in New York city two out of every five children are being raised in households with incomes below the poverty level: that means that 40 per cent of New York's children live in households where a choice must be made each month between paying the landlord to avoid eviction and homelessness, or feeding the children.

Across the nation, the plight of children is not much better: statistically, one in four US children faces the same horrific fate of living in poverty. And then there are homeless youth. Some estimates say that nearly 500,000 young, rootless Americans who are not yet adults but who no longer have family, are currently homeless. These are the maturing children of poverty. They are uneducated, desperate and largely ignored by government — until they are apprehended at some crime.

## FEDERAL INACTION
In recent years, as the number of homeless Americans increased dramatically, the response of the federal government has been minimal. Increasingly, advocates and local officials are looking towards Washington for help in con-

trolling a problem national in scale. And, under the present administration, Washington has looked away. Not only has it failed to address the needs of the homeless, but administration policies and cutbacks in programmes have greatly exacerbated the problem.

For fifty-three years in the United States, the federal government played a leading role in the creation of housing for poor people. Federally subsidised housing has been cut with a radical fervour by more than 75 per cent since 1981. Waiting lists for these programmes are several years long — if they have not already been 'frozen'. In his budget for 1987, President Reagan proposed eliminating all new funding for subsidised housing. Without housing, there is no solution for the homeless.

During the same period that the gap between the need for housing and the supply of housing has widened, the ability of poor people to compete for that housing has been crippled. Welfare grants to families with children have been cut by $3.6 billion since 1981, and the monthly caseload in the United States has been reduced by 442,000 persons. In 1984, only fifty-five out of every hundred poor children were receiving welfare benefits.

While many poor people are forced to go without shelter, others cling to their housing and scrimp on food. Yet, the Reagan administration has harmed those people too. Federal food programmes have been slashed dramatically. Since 1982, $6.8 billion has been cut from the food stamp programme, the national nutrition programme that gives poor people vouchers with which to purchase groceries.

Even the 'truly needy', to use President Reagan's discredited term, have been brutalised by Washington's social agenda of the 1980s. Many physically and mentally disabled persons have brutally been cast out onto the streets. The purging of eligible elderly and disabled recipients from the social security roll has had a devastating effect. As a consequence, a mentally ill person who loses his income will — in short order — lose whatever shelter he had. That adds one more number to the ranks of the homeless.

In addition, a federal promise of 2000 community mental health facilities has resulted in less than 800 that have actually been established. Studies show that up to one-third of the homeless are mentally ill, yet they receive little or no mental health care.

Obviously, it is time that the policies of the United States government start addressing the needs of its poorest citizens. There are solutions, but they need a federal initiative. For mental health care, community-based services are

40

needed. To prevent homelessness, tenants in public housing need assistance to avert impending evictions. In the long run, the United States must make more federal funds available to promote low-income housing in both urban and rural areas of the country.

## THE NATIONAL COALITION FOR THE HOMELESS
Like the Simon community in Ireland, the National Coalition and its members combine direct service work with political campaigning. The National Coalition is a nationwide organisation which takes as its credo that decent shelter, sufficient food and affordable housing must be fundamental rights in any society that calls itself civilised. The National Coalition has gained court rulings on the rights of homeless persons to shelter. It monitors federal programmes developed to assist the poor. It provides technical assistance to shelter and housing providers across the country, and has recently secured the enactment of the first major federal legislation to aid the homeless.

## THE BATTLE PLAN
The community of activists that work with the homeless in the United States have long agreed that a three-tiered solution to homelessness is needed. The pressing, immediate need of course is *emergency shelter*. Such shelters must be safe, accessible and respectful of a person's human dignity. Emergency relief is desperately needed to preserve lives, while more substantial solutions are developed.

But shelter is only a first step to a remedy. A second tier of relief, what some people call *transitional housing*, is also needed. The point of transitional housing is to offer relatively short-term but intensive assistance beyond just food and shelter to a homeless person.

The range of second-tier services will vary widely. Some mentally ill homeless persons require psychiatric intervention to stabilise their conditions. Other homeless persons, addicted to drugs or alcohol, need rehabilitation. Many homeless young people need an intensive regimen of job training or remedial education to enable them to live independently.

But transitional housing cannot succeed when there is no third-tier housing: *affordable permanent housing*. In the United States there is a drastic shortfall of beds at all three tiers of the analysis. Yet the absolute shortage of permanent housing frustrates the success of even the limited tier one and tier two programmes.

## BATTLE TACTICS
The president of the United States says he thinks homeless people live on

the streets by choice — a clearly insensitive and wrong comment — and the opportunity to educate the public (and denounce the president's housing policies) is created. In the United States a movement has developed over the past few years, and a methodology of advocacy has been developed, although only in hindsight.

In the late 1970s homelessness was beginning to ripen into a crisis, but neither the public nor the media, nor the political establishment was paying much attention. Yet the problem was growing and the misery of the homeless was real.

Finding no political interest in aiding the homeless, a group of researchers, and a lawyer (the individuals who later formed the Coalition for the Homeless) took to the courts in New York city. The lawyer identified provisions in New York law that might support a legal claim that the homeless have a right to shelter, and the researchers examined both the causes and scale of homelessness, as well as remedies.

That work led to the filing of the now celebrated lawsuit *Callahan* v. *Carey*, the first case in the United States to recognise a right to shelter for the homeless poor. In that suit, the New York supreme court ordered the New York governor, Hugh Carey, and mayor, Edward Koch, to provide shelter and board to every homeless man who requested it.

The first step, then, in what became a national advocacy campaign, was a successful lawsuit. But court injunctions only go so far. And the shelter provided under the *Callahan* suit in New York created problems. Basically, the Koch-established shelter system institutionalised barbaric human warehouses. Many homeless people quite rationally shun these institutions for the streets.

But more fundamental was the fact that shelters are not what homeless people really need. Housing, jobs and a decent income are the true cures. So the battle had to continue.

What the *Callahan* litigation provided was a forum for teaching the American public about the causes and consequences of homelessness. Suddenly, the issue had legitimacy. And in an odd way so too did homeless people.

What litigation did is shift the terms of the debate. The homeless could no longer merely be viewed as idle beggars, worthy of disdain, sympathy or perhaps charity. The *Callahan* lawsuit made the homeless aggrieved citizens demanding, in the courts, not charity but justice. It was a subtle point at first, but one which became the cornerstone of a continuing campaign.

The Coalition for the Homeless turned its gaze beyond the courts and into a full-scale effort to win the hearts and minds of the people. That meant clarifying issues simply so the news media could become the instrument of education.

Politicians by and large were ignored at this stage of the effort. A near universal truth about politicians (Ireland's Senator Brendan Ryan may well be the exception) is that they will almost never respond to human need, but will almost always respond to political pressure. Rather than squandering energy on the politicians, we worked to engage a constituency that would demand relief for the homeless.

That meant shifting press attention away from the eccentric stories about the homeless woman with a million dollars in her shopping bags, and to the real causes of homelessness. It was essential to force a public awareness that homelessness was not merely the result of limitations, disabilities or contrariness of homeless people. Homelessness had to be seen for what it is: the forseeable consequence of deliberate public policy decisions by government officials. Once that was made clear the press could take notice.

And the dramatic confrontation needed for the media was always at hand. To juxtapose the homeless man, woman or child — either in print or television — next to the architect of the policies that rendered the person homeless, offered dramatic and lucid pictures. Like all good drama, it taught quite effectively a message: there are not only victims, but there are villains. And most important of all, there are solutions.

**PUBLIC CONSENSUS CHANGES**
In a reasonably short period, the media campaign bore fruit. Suddenly, in places like Los Angeles and New York there were major political demands to create shelter and housing for the homeless. By 1986 New York city was spending nearly a quarter of a billion dollars on shelter alone.

By the spring of 1987, national polls found that 68 per cent of Americans thought the federal government should spend more funds on the homeless. And even in the comparatively conservative southern states, homelessness is becoming one of the major issues in state capitals, according to other polls. Overwhelmingly, *knowledge* about homelessness is being translated into *support* for creating housing for the homeless.

43

The public support did translate into a major political victory in early 1987. Forced with mounting public indignation over the homeless, a bi-partisan coalition of members of congress rushed a nearly $500 million authorisation to help the homeless through the house and senate, over President Reagan's objections. For the first time the federal government is accepting a modest, but not insignificant, responsibility in assisting America's homeless.

## SURVIVAL ACT

At the same time, support is building for national legislation, prepared by the National Coalition, which would put the federal government in a position of seriously demonstrating its intent to end homelessness.

The Homeless Persons Survival Act of 1987, with a $4 billion price tag, is an omnibus bill that breaks down into three major areas. The first area covers the emergency needs of people already homeless. The bill would create a national right to shelter, and would make a host of other existing welfare programmes available to the homeless. The balance of the legislation would enact a number of measures to prevent homelessness, including various anti-eviction and displacement laws. In addition, the Survival Act would reinstate and improve a number of long-range programmes designed to increase the availability of low cost housing.

Turning to the needs of homeless youth, the Survival Act would increase dramatically funding for the nation's existing runaway and homeless youth programme. Currently the programme funds 265 centres around the country which serve primarily as referral centres for homeless youth. Referrals for homeless youth tend to be futile when there are no resources to which young people can be referred. The Survival Act recognises this and would provide up to $50 million in funding to create residences for homeless youth that could provide education and job training in addition to meeting the survival needs of the young people.

## HOMELESS YOUTH IN NEW YORK

A local advocacy effort that focused on forcing New York city to aid homeless youth demonstrates both the methodology and the frustration of advocacy. In late 1983 the Coalition for the Homeless and a number of allied organisations issued a searing study entitled *Homeless youth in New York City: nowhere to turn*. The report attacked the 'piecemeal' government response to homelessness among the city's young people:

> In New York City there are emergency shelter beds equal in number to just one per cent of the estimated 20,000 young people annually in need of shelter, . . . many of these homeless youth are among the

thousands of children in recent years discharged from foster care to their own responsibility.

Typically, the study said, the homeless youth are 'poor children, often from broken homes, enmeshed in a web of poverty, whose childhoods were usually characterised by parental unemployment, bad health and grossly sub-standard employment.'

The report gained wide distribution, and various municipal officials pledged to take steps to remedy at least some of the problems. Meanwhile, the number of young people living in city shelters for the homeless and on the streets continues to increase.

## TO THE COURTS
Ultimately, the officials broke their promises and by 1984 it was plain that they intended to do as little as possible for homeless youth. The Coalition and its allies returned to the courts. Earlier in the 1980s the Coalition had successfully argued that a state could not eject a mentally ill person from a psychiatric hospital and abandon that person to city streets. A corrupt mental health system had made it routine practice to fail in its attempt to teach independence to patients while hospitalised, and then to dump the patients without help in the community. Homelessness — and phsyical and mental deterioration — followed.

The same thing was happening to young people who were being dumped — unprepared for independence — out of the city's child-care system. Typically, at the age of eighteen, a young person would be told to leave — and that would be it. In many cases the children were improperly encouraged to leave foster care at an earlier age, normally at the time they became disruptive to the agency being paid to provide the foster care.

The Coalition went to court, and the courts found the city was acting illegally. Basically, the courts ruled that foster care agencies — acting *in loco parentis* — had an obligation to teach basic life skills to children entrusted to their care. The courts also held that discharge from foster care to independent living had to be a gradual thing. When troubles develop for the young person, the court ruled, there must be some support from the agencies that discharged that child.

At long last there appears to be some movement to at least stem the growing tide of homeless youth.

## CONTINUING THE STRUGGLE
All the skirmishes around homelessness are doomed to ultimate failure until the battle for sufficient housing is won. There is no solution to homelessness in America without sufficient, affordable housing. That is where the struggle will continue.

by Robert M. Hayes

# Living Nowhere: A Child's Life on the Streets in New York City — the Covenant House Approach

New York city is a well-known centre for much of the world's business, banking and telecommunications industries. New York enjoys a rich cultural life of music, art, ballet and theatre, but next to the lights on Broadway are the marquees of the pornographic bookstores, massage parlours and transient hotels. Times Square is the unofficial red light district, where there is wholesale buying and selling of children and youth.

On any given night in New York city, police estimate that there are up to 10,000 runaway and homeless children of sixteen years and under. The Federal Department of Health and Human Services estimates that there are a million and a half children, aged seventeen and under, who leave their homes each year, and a recent Congressional Report estimates there are up to 500,000 homeless disconnected youth between the ages of sixteen and twenty-one. The numbers are staggering: one child or youth living on the streets of a city already represents a tragic statistic.

## WHO ARE THESE KIDS?
Here are some statistics on some of the kids that have come through the Covenant House residential programme in the Times Square area of New York.

Among the 8600 children that came through the Covenant House New York programme last year, the male—female ratio was two to one. In general, the ethnicity of the homeless youth population reflects the ethnic distribution of the population in the area where they are served. In New York, 58 per cent were black, 27 per cent were Hispanic, 15 per cent were white or other.

About 60 per cent of the kids come from New York metropolitan area and about 20 per cent come from neighbouring counties.

Fifty-eight per cent of our kids in New York were eighteen years old and over. The next largest percentage were those aged sixteen to seventeen. In general, most of the youth living on the street are sixteen to twenty-one

47

years old. They are growing too old for both the child welfare and juvenile justice systems.

Close to 60 per cent of the youth in our shelters at Covenant House have had previous foster care, mental health or juvenile justice placements. Over 75 per cent of the kids are high school dropouts. Many have a third or fourth grade reading level.

Over 80 per cent of our runaway and homeless youth suffer from extreme emotional depression. Fifty per cent have attempted suicide or consider it their only option.

Fifty per cent of them have been the victims of repeated physical abuse. Over 25 per cent of our girls have admitted to being raped at some time in their lives.

Most of the kids lived in poor and deteriorating family situations. Close to 80 per cent lived in single-parent female-headed households that are poor. More than 50 per cent of our youth come from homes where drug and alcohol abuse is prevalent. Only 12 per cent of the youth in the residence are able to or want to return home.

### WHAT SERVICES EXIST?
In New York city, the Department of Social Service, Children's Division, called Special Services for Children, provides care for 17,000 children from babies to eighteen years. These children live in various foster care, group home and institutional facilities throughout the five boroughs of the city. For runaway and homeless youth between the ages of sixteen and twenty-one years, there are approximately 444 beds in New York city. These beds are in transitional living programmes, runaway homeless youth programmes, residential crisis services, and a parent-child programme.

These programmes exist because of recent local, state and federal initiatives funded by the Department of Social Services, Youth Bureau, Department of Labour and Juvenile Justice and Delinquency Prevention Acts. The programmes are usually run by private, voluntary, alternative youth service agencies that chart their history back to the 1960s.

A number of these private agencies have organised state and local coalitions and have developed, with county and state governments, innovative programme models. Services include both paid and volunteer 'host' foster homes for emergency child placements, short-term alternative group homes, court diversion projects, and small community-based transitional living apartments, in order to prepare the older youth for independent living.

48

The primary benefits of the alternative youth-care programme models include the provision of attractive, community-based, low-cost residential and social services to a multi-problem population that has often fallen between the cracks of the existing child welfare and juvenile justice system. The deficiencies of the alternative youth services are that services and funding continue to follow a 'problem focus' (Moses 1978). A youth who returns to the same centre for more than a year could be classified for purposes of funding, as a 'runaway, abused and neglected, drug or alcohol-dependent, delinquent, hustler or prostitute'. The second deficiency is funding. State and federal grants (depending on the number of children and their problems, the location and the type of facility) cover between 50 and 80 per cent of the real costs of programme operation. This has caused, among other things, the opening and closing of many centres; high staff turnover; inadequate therapeutic care at times; and the formation of coalitions and advocacy groups more involved with new funding patterns than with social justice issues concerning the poor. However, all of the existing services only meet a fraction of the need.

## A SYSTEMS MODEL OF RESIDENTIAL CARE: COVENANT HOUSE
All told, throughout all of its centres last year, Covenant House provided full residential and social services to over 12,000 homeless children and youth. With variations, this model has been replicated in urban programmes in Toronto, Fort Lauderdale and Houston. The programme model has also been successfully replicated in different cultures, notably Guatemala and Panama.

The theoretical framework of a systems model of adolescent care requires, by definition, that the agency provides internally, or through its external linkages, a comprehensive, holistic therapeutic approach that addresses the multiple problems of homeless youth. The multiple problems are dealt with according to an appropriate analysis of the hierarchy of the youngsters' needs ie their physical needs (food, clothes, medical attention) and their needs for safety (through shelter and protection from the 'street'). After these most immediate needs are met, all agency departments then attempt (through various counselling, therapeutic, educational and work programmes) to meet the adolescents' psycho-social and self-esteem needs at that time, as well as making initial approaches to the process of self-actualisation that each person will strive to achieve in his/her life (Maslow 1962).

The second theoretical underpinning of this systems model is that the adolescent social service agency must be the bridge between the 'alternative' and the 'institutional' — ie between those alternative agencies that only provide for immediate, emergency needs, or who attempt only to change immediate, present behavioural patterns; and those institutions and traditional analytic therapies that work over long periods of time only on psycho-social and self-esteem needs with their clients, to the exclusion of any emergency or short-term assistance to an at-risk population.

Covenant House is such an alternative institution. It was founded in 1968 by a Franciscan priest and a group of his friends as a response to the tremendous needs of the homeless and runaway children who were living in abandoned buildings, apartment 'crash pads', and parks in East Greenwich Village.

The Covenant House programme, in the first four years of its operation, consisted of a half-dozen highly motivated and inexperienced volunteers who lived and worked in tenement apartments at or near the facility, and who cared for homeless children on an around-the-clock basis. Immediate services (food, clothing, shelter and counselling) were provided by the staff for approximately fifteen children at a time. Relationships were built with other local service providers, especially hospitals and free clinics, in order to obtain needed medical and psychiatric care. During the early period of programme development, the staff dedication, values and hours worked were high. The salaries and benefits were low. The average staff 'life' before fatigue, illness and 'burnout' was about six months. A standing joke of some staff at the agency was 'The salary is so low, you have to borrow money to leave.'

Because of the ever-increasing numbers of young people who came for help, and because of their great need for medical and dental care, education and training and, for some, their need for longer-term residential care, an alternative care model needed to be developed. From 1972 to the present, Covenant House has been developing various programme models of therapeutic residential care for this population. The residential and administrative models have been built on the early experiences of the free clinics, hotlines, and emergency shelters. Early stages of this agency's development entailed a growth from a shelter for fifteen children in various small apartments on New York's Lower East Side to a module of ten group homes (residential facilities for up to twelve children, staffed by five adults, with social work, medical and psychological backup services) spread throughout New York city. This programme provided emergency and short-term care for approximately 120 children.

In 1977, the agency opened its first residential and clinical multiservice centre in the heart of Times Square — a major catchment area for the over-whelming number of homeless children and youths who come to this section, both from other parts of the city and from various places around the country. The outreach part of the centre is located on Eighth Avenue, on a block designated the 'Minnesota Strip'. The other part of the facility is three blocks from Times Square, and has within it a residence for up to 200 youngsters (divided into sections of twenty-five to thirty children), a medical and psychological clinic, a soup kitchen, and an educational/vocational centre. The centre in New York has treated on an emergency and short-term basis approximately 10,000 children and youths a year, ranging in age from twenty-one years to three weeks old.

Central to the development of this programme model has been the agency's principles and practices of residential care. These principles are taught in orientation and staff training sessions for all residential and clinical staff, and are the framework for various individual and group treatment modalities. The five principles of operation of the centre are: immediacy, sanctuary, values, structure, and choice.

*Immediacy*. The centre is located in the area of need, within walking distance of the bus terminal and the arcades on Forty-second Street. Immediacy means that the centre is open twenty-four hours a day, seven days a week. It also means that counsellors practise immediacy through an 'open intake': no youth is turned away on his or her first time at the centre. Each youngster is accepted and offered immediate services (food, clothes, shower and shelter) through a specially trained intake team. The children are not under pressure to appear 'motivated' to enter the programme.

The second principle of operation is *sanctuary*, or safety. This aspect has to do with the entire environment of care that the young person experiences. Sanctuary, by definition, is a refuge or place of safety. Counsellors are selected and trained to ensure that each young person is protected from the dangers of the street. Each youngster is protected also from any harsh judgements concerning his or her past. In time, with care, patience, and diagnostic shrewdness, the personal histories unfold.

Sanctuary also means that the centre is a clean and comfortable environment for all the youths. Plants, bright carpets, and comfortable furniture help to re-establish in each person a sense of dignity and self-worth:

> As Raymond passed through the lounge area with one of the volunteer counsellors, Brian, a 19-year-old who had been coming to the centre for six months for a job training group, thought he recognised Raymond from the street. Being one of the 'older' youths, he tried to establish himself with Raymond with the words, 'Hey, man, how ya doin? Don't I know you? Where did you get those pants? Phew! You stink!' Raymond, feeling accused

51

and vulnerable in front of the others, turned and started to attack Brian verbally. The counsellor in charge of the group immediately separated the two young men, reminded them both of the rules and procedures, and then asked Raymond to go upstairs to the clothing room. Turning to Brian, he said, 'Brian, that wasn't very funny. He's new. Please keep that kind of humour to yourself.' Brian responded immediately, 'But he does stink.' These incidents repeat themselves daily.

The next principle of operation is *value communication*. Each person in the centre is asked to tell the truth, to care about him/herself, to respect others, and to start working on plans of activity with counsellors and social workers. Each youth in the intake and diagnostic sessions is told that the rules and procedures (no drugs or alcohol; no use of violence, verbal or physical; and 'be human') are parts of a value system that is different from the value system of the street and of some of the institutions that these youngsters have visited:

By the third day Maria and the treatment team were more and more uncomfortable with Anne/Susan's progress. 'Susan,' a 13-year-old runaway who came to the centre three nights ago, would not call home to let her parents know she was safe; and the address of her 'aunt' in Hartford could not be verified. Anne was getting restless. The team thought she might walk out of the door, defence-less, because this was her first time in New York. That night Brenda, a specialty social worker, called her by name 'Susan' when she was in a small group. For a brief moment, Anne did not react, then almost too quickly responded, 'Yes?' Brenda asked her to come into the office, took a breath, looked at the young woman, and said, 'That's not your real name, is it?' At first angry, then scared, then silent, the girl refused to answer. Brenda in a strong way reminded her of her promise to tell the truth while at the centre. With a direct intensity, Brenda told her of all parents' concern for their child, even if there have been problems. Then Brenda told 'Susan' what was on her mind: that when a person lives a lie, she needs eventually to leave those to whom she has lied. She told her that she knew she was thinking of leaving, and that if she did, her chances of finding help on the street were slim. Brenda then asked 'Susan' again if they could both call her mother, and that she would be there for the talk. The girl stared at Brenda for a long moment, and said quietly, 'You're right.' Then she said, 'I'll call, but I don't want to go home.' Brenda answered, 'Thank you. But let's take one step at a time. What's your name?'

52

The fourth principle of the therapeutic relationship is *structure*. The structures of a residential programme are the parameters of the individual and group relationships, as well as the rituals and accountability systems for the rules and procedures in the centre. In time, each youth, together with the therapeutic team, is responsible for working out a realistic, short-term plan for him/herself — a return home or to school, or to start preparing for a job and eventual independent living.

The fifth principle is *choice* — the awareness and knowledge of options, and the opportunity to select alternatives that will bring about growth and development. Within the principle of choice is the encouragement, and at times the confrontation, by the counselling staff in order to help the young people break their destructive choices for the 'street', and to support their choices towards the 'good':

> It took about two weeks for Raymond to deteriorate. Although he understood the rules against violence and provocation, he did not understand the banter and verbal jousts of the other residents in the house. More than that, he didn't understand his rage at not being able to spell. On Friday, he received the results of the Armed Forces' literacy test. He failed. Raymond came in late for dinner, thought that Billy was staring at him, and taunted, 'You wanna fight?' Billy, having finished his dinner, laughed, and responded, 'Sure.' Raymond threw his plate at Billy and screamed, 'Come on! I don't care! I'll kill you!' Mike, the shift supervisor, came over, separated the two, and immediately said to the older youth, 'Bill, leave the room. Now. This has nothing to do with you. Go. I'll talk to you later.'
>
> Without touching Raymond, and while standing between him and the other youth, Mike said, 'Let's go into the office, Ray.' 'No, you don't care! The hell with all of you. I'll kill you! You want to call the cops. You want me in the hospital. That's what the shrink said yesterday, huh? All I want is to go in the Army, I want to go into the Army.' Mike, in a firm, but unchallenging voice said, 'Ray, you know what you are doing. This is the fifth incident since you've been here. We can't have you threatening people. Ray, will you let me call . . .' 'No! You won't call the police!' Raymond transfixed Mike with his cold, blue stare. Mike stepped slightly to the side, and back a step. 'Ray . . .' And as Mike was beginning to speak, Raymond took a chair and threw it. He then bolted out the door. Mike followed the youth outside, spoke to the outside counsellor and the security guard. 'Please write up a discharge card

on Raymond. If he returns, he may not get back in. The most we can do is refer him to the hospital.'

Not all young people are available for assistance when they first enter. Some need to return many times before they will accept help.

### FUNDING AND IMPLEMENTATION
The need to maintain and augment funding, in order to ensure the agency's survival while it attempts to fulfil its internal goals and objectives is one of the major dilemmas facing every voluntary, alternative youth agency today. The agency must relate to individuals in the community; local, state, and federal governments; and business and political groups. It would take a separate article, however, to analyse adequately an agency's position and relationship to these groups, especially when there appears to be conflict between an agency's goals and its own economic and programmatic survival. However, a cursory analysis shows that, unlike the majority of agencies in the United States that care for runaway youth, Covenant House raises over 90 per cent of its operating budget from the private sector (individual gifts and contributions, a mailing list, and corporate grants). Less than 10 per cent of its support comes from the city, state or federal government.

The number of homeless children and the varied nature of their problems demand that the staff are supported in maintaining a high degree of energy, care, dedication and diagnostic knowledge concerning behavioural traits and character disorders in adolescents. This combination of sensitivity, knowledge and action must be coupled with strong administrative supports and supervision. This model of care is effective because its principles and practices of operation (immediacy, sanctuary, value communication, structure, and choice) provide a total environment within which various treatment modalities — short- and long-term, individual, group and family — can interact and complement each other.

### NEXT STEPS
In April 1987, 100 representatives from non-governmental organisations (NGOs) and from UNICEF's staff convened a workshop at the United Nations on Shelter for the Homeless: Problems related to Children in their Family Environment. Our charge at this forum was to make recommendations to UNICEF's board of directors, to assist them as they develop their priorities for the world's children.

Thus, in partnersnip with UNICEF and governments, we make the following recommendations:

- UNICEF should continue to make homeless streetchildren a major part of its policies and programmes to the end of this century. Presently there are over 100 million streetchildren, and their plight worsens daily.

- All services to homeless children should be put in the context of family; and that we as a society (governments, UNICEF, and NGOs) work to support the family through appropriate policies and programmes.

- Support to children and family must include child and maternal health; access to land and adequate housing (both emergency and long-term), particularly in urban centres; education, day care and child care; and employment and training opportunities, especially for women who are heads of households.

- NGOs need to collaborate with each other and with UNICEF to help governments develop a stronger political consensus to provide adequate housing, income and support to at-risk children and families.

- There should be greater educational outreach in our communities on sexual responsibility, with special emphasis on male attitudes toward family.

- UNICEF should continue to research the numbers and needs of at-risk children, with a particular focus on the growing number of young girls on the street.

- And finally, we should help to empower at-risk children and families so that they can continue to create for themselves solutions and positive changes in the communities where they choose to live.

by Stephen F. Torkelsen

### Bibliography

EDELMAN, MARIAN WRIGHT. *A Children's Defense Budget*. Washington, D.C.: Children's Defense Fund, 1987.

FREUDENBERGER, H.J. & TORKELSEN, S.E. Beyond the Interpersonal: A Systems Model of Therapeutic Care for Homeless Children and Youth. *Psychotherapy* 1984, 21(1).

INDEPENDENT COMMISSION ON INTERNATIONAL HUMANITARIAN ISSUES. *Street Children: A Growing Urban Tragedy*. London: Weidenfeld & Nicolson, 1986.

MASLOW, ABRAHAM H. *Toward a Psychology of Being*. Princeton, N.J.: D. Van Nostrand, 1962.

MOSES, A.B. The Runaway Youth Act: Paradoxes of Reform. *Social Service Review* 1978, 52(2), 227-43.

NEW YORK STATE COUNCIL ON CHILDREN & FAMILIES. *Meeting the Needs of Homeless Youth: A Report of the Homeless Youth Steering Committee*. Albany, N.Y.: State of New York, 1984.

NON-GOVERNMENTAL ORGANIZATIONS COMMITTEE ON UNICEF. *Recommendations of the working group on 'Shelter for the Homeless: Problems Related to Children in their Family Environment'*. New York, N.Y.: April, 1987.

TOWBER, RICHARD I. *Characteristics of Homeless Families*. New York, N.Y.: Human Resources Administration, 1985.

UNICEF. The State of the World's Children: A Statistical Picture. *The 1987 State of the World's Children Report*, 1987, Chapters 3 and 4.

# Streetchildren — Key Issues in the European Perspective

Homelessness is a complex issue that touches many areas, including housing, education, unemployment, family and social networks and other socio-economic issues, all of which interlock at some points. Homelessness among the young knows no geographical boundaries, and is certainly not restricted to Third World or developing countries. The industrial nations are equally concerned about this problem, but appear to be generally at a loss as to either the causes or the solutions. It seems that the further one investigates this matter, the more confusing the picture becomes.

At a European level, we have to take into account the various local, regional and national circumstances, policies and practices, and to identify certain key social and cultural features.

## SOCIAL FACTORS — THE BREAKDOWN OF THE FAMILY UNIT

In a recent study carried out by the Commission of the European Communities, it was found that 17 per cent of fifteen-to-twenty-four-year-olds do not live in a family framework. There appears also to be an increasing trend towards the creation of smaller households, which are being led by people younger than in previous generations. And it was found that since divorce has been on the increase, children and young people are affected by the changes and rearrangements that marriage breakdown causes and it is children who suffer. Single parents are also increasing, and they are vulnerable to economic or cultural stresses, which can lead to family breakdown. The evidence from people working in the field is that home is not always a good place to be, and it is increasingly apparent that in certain European countries, people are leaving home at a younger age. It is also clearly evident that emotional, physical or sexual abuse by family members features more frequently in the case histories of homeless young people.

All of these factors contribute to an increase in the number of young single people looking for accommodation. The ability to cope of many of these young people is certainly affected by their personal experiences, which are now more likely than ever to include abuse, rejection and abandonment by their families.

Of course circumstances differ from country to country, and from the evidence that is available in northern European countries, the traditional family is losing ground, whereas in Portugal, for example, and possibly southern Italy, there is still a very strong sense of the family.

## THE FAILURE OF INSTITUTIONAL CARE
Evidence is beginning to emerge that many young people who become homeless will have been at some time in institutional care or will have been involved with preventative services in some way during their childhood. Increasingly these institutions have either failed to identify the risks of long-term homelessness faced by the young person, or have failed to prepare the young person adequately for transition from institutional care to independent accommodation.

## INADEQUATE HOUSING POLICIES
It is also clear from our knowledge of the European countries that government policies on housing have not yet developed to meet the increased demand for housing by single people, and for housing suitable for shared use by single people. As a consequence, many young people are limited to those areas of housing which are rejected by the population as a whole. This has led to a creation of ghettoes in certain open areas, and the proliferation of squatting, particularly in the Netherlands and Britain. To make matters worse, the amount of privately rented accommodation has dwindled over the past ten to fifteen years, and in any case it is usually beyond the financial means of young people who are unemployed or on low earnings.

## DEFINITIONS AND STATISTICS
The European Parliament Social Affairs Committee recognises three categories of people affected by homelessness:

- those who are actually homeless
- those who are threatened with homelessness
- those who are potentially threatened with homelessness.

Actually homeless people are single people and couples who live without housing or permanent shelter and who have no permanent residence, people who are sometimes referred to as 'vagrants'. Single people threatened with homelessness are those who are about to lose their present accommodation and who are unable to secure permanent housing. And the third group, those potentially threatened with homelessness, are people whose present accommodation is totally inadequate and insecure, and who would not be reaccommodated if they lost their present accommodation.

The definitions of young people vary from country to country in Europe, and legal rights of access to public and private housing are also different in every single European country and are not clearly formulated. The legislation of member states of the European communities has created a jungle of special provisions with little consistency.

There are no real statistics on homeless people and in particular on young homeless people, but the estimate is that there are between a million and a million and a half people actually homeless in Europe, and that at least 10 per cent of the population of the European community are threatened or potentially threatened with homelessness.

## ECONOMIC CHANGE AND HOUSING POLICY
The media image of the young 'runaway' or the young 'throwaway' certainly reflects reality up to a point, but over the eleven years that I have worked in the field, the traditional situation of young people has changed, and the typical profile of a young homeless person has also changed. In many European and other countries, a young person who is homeless is often affected by features of society such as unemployment, poor training and educational facilities, lack of access to the everyday services such as health and housing.

The image of the young homeless person of the 1960s and 1970s has changed, and now, as the World Health Organisation pointed out in its report of 1985, the risk behaviour of young people is seen more as an expression of their search for a new lifestyle: the expectations of young people have been downgraded.

The majority of young people who now seek independent accommodation are unemployed. Housing schemes that were designed on the assumption that many of the residents would be out at work all day are no longer suitable in times of unemployment, and even when young people can find accommodation it is often in isolated highrise buildings without community resources and often a long way from suitable social activities. There is an increasing tendency, even in the voluntary sector, to house young unemployed people in ghettoes, because the authorities who give planning approval would be unlikely to give approval to schemes in the so-called acceptable residential areas. In its true sense 'social housing' should mean finding accommodation for people in need of shelter within the existing community. This is the only way to prevent a sense of alienation. Good examples of this are to be found in Denmark and the Netherlands.

## WELFARE POLICIES
This is a particularly complex area, as every single country in the European

community has its own welfare policy. Most European governments have not developed — or indeed are now demolishing — social security systems which at least offer a kind of safety net for the young unemployed person. This, together with a policy of spending inadequate amounts on housing at an affordable price for young people, and the drying up of accommodation in the private rented sector, has caused immense problems. Whether any government in the European community is prepared to make the capital investment to solve these problems remains to be seen.

### A STRATEGY OF PREVENTION NEEDED
Neither the welfare services nor the housing programmes of the European countries take into account the new demand from young homeless people. Nor has the breakdown of the traditional family structure been taken into account. What we are seeing is a kind of discrimination against young people who do not conveniently fit into traditional patterns of work and family. It is no accident that when one is looking in the legislation of the European Parliament for the words 'youth homelessness', one comes up against the term 'marginalisation' time and time again.

Unless we undertake a strategy of prevention in Europe, we are likely as a society to pay the price for such short-sightedness. I have seen evidence of what can go wrong in cities such as Chicago and New York. There, the alienation has gone several steps further, as evidenced by the amount of violence in these cities.

### A BLUEPRINT FOR THE FUTURE
The European Young Homeless Group has made a number of recommendations some of which we hope will be included in the new Social Affairs' Committee Report to the European Parliament. These are as follows:

1 That comprehensive social policy should be developed with special regard to young people

2 That youth housing should be included in all government housing policies

3 That homeless young people should be given the fullest protection within the legal framework of each country

4 That those homeless young people who are unemployed should be provided with adequate housing and welfare subsidies in order to maintain a quality of life which does not exclude them from the mainstream of society

5  That the promotion of the above four points should be encouraged amongst the member states

6  That an exchange of research and information on all problems concerning youth homelessness should be promoted between governments, non-government organisations and youth organisations

7  That the commission should support and finance organisation to include all the associations working on behalf of the homeless in the member states, so that the development of the above policies can be co-ordinated throughout Europe

by Nic Fenton

# THE
# SITUATION
# IN IRELAND

# Children and Young People Out-of-Home in Ireland

Children can become homeless anywhere in the world because of any of a number of tragic circumstances:

- natural disaster such as flood, fire, earthquake
- economic failure of their country, resulting in famine, poverty, lack of shelter and housing programmes and unemployment
- war, the threat of conflict or actual armed violence
- special care which they require not being provided either within the family or by the state
- being neglected or abused by their families

## THE SITUATION IN IRELAND

In Ireland we have had experience of all these tragic circumstances, many of which still exist in the developing countries — famine, malnutrition, abandoned children, high infant and child mortality rates, child slavery. In the eighteenth and nineteenth centuries, hundreds and thousands of children were lost or unaccounted for in Ireland.[1]

It was these homeless children who formed the very basis of the Irish child-care system which we have today. The nineteenth-century provision for children ranged from foundling hospitals to charter schools, work-houses, reformatory schools and industrial schools, and there were also privately funded institutions. The 1908 Children's Act brought some improvements and greater protection for children and the regularisation of industrial and reformatory school systems. The 1908 Children's Act continues to be the main legislation which governs our child-care system and services in Ireland. In fact, for the sixty years following the passing of the Act, there was scarcely any discussion on the child-care and children's services.

## CHANGES, GOOD AND BAD

The Tuaraim Report (1966), the Kennedy Report (1970) and the Task Force Report (1980) all highlighted the many deficiencies in the existing

65

child-care services, particularly the need for preventative services to enable children to stay in their own home and environment and the reform of the children's services and related legislation. Many improvements were in fact made during this period:

- development of group homes

- training of child-care workers

- increased numbers of social workers for family support

- assessment centres and special schools for children in trouble with the law

The Department of Health and the regional health boards undertook responsibility for most of the residential and non-residential services for children. The Department of Education continued its responsibility for reformatory schools, now designated as special schools, and helped to develop a community-based youth work service through Comhairle le Leas Óige (the Youth Service Board). The probation and welfare service in particular and the juvenile liaison scheme were developed and expanded by the Department of Justice. It is perhaps understandable that many people assumed that with better preventative care there would be less reason for taking children into care in the first place and, with improved child-care facilities for children from childhood to sixteen years of age, that all our children would be cared for. However, this assumption is invalid, and these expectations have not been met.

The resources to provide a comprehensive service for children from childhood to sixteen years have not been made available. Social workers' priority is for providing care and protection for younger children and babies. This is clearly indicated by the percentage of younger children who are placed in care (see below).

Major changes have taken place in the area of residential care over the last twenty years:

- *The large institutions have disappeared.*

- The *number of residential homes was reduced* from three reformatories, thirty-one 'industrial' schools and forty-two private institutions in 1969, to t  o assessment centres, three special schools and thirty-three children's hon  s in 1983.[2]

- The *number of children in care* has dropped from 3993 in industrial and private institutions in May 1969 to 2534 in December 1983 (53 per cent of whom were in foster care).[3]

66

- But the age range of children in care has also changed. In 1969 50 per cent of the 3993 children in care were over twelve years and 24 per cent were over fourteen years,[4] whereas of new admissions in 1983, 50 per cent were under two years, 11 per cent over twelve years and only 3 per cent were over fifteen years.[5]

So, we now have fewer institutions and fewer children in care, but the great majority of children in care are babies and younger children. Preventative services have not been developed to provide support for families in their local communities. Because of a lack of resources the social work service is primarily geared to cope with crises with children and families. The health boards have not been able to facilitate preventative work and community participation in service, planning and delivery.

Not only has the number of residential places for older children decreased but the absence of day activities for children over five years is in marked contrast to what has been provided for under-fives. We have four Youth Encounter Schemes and three Neighbourhood Youth Schemes throughout the whole country, which can scarcely be regarded as sufficient for our older children.

As the changes were implemented, attention was almost totally focused on the younger children, to the detriment of the older children. It is difficult to imagine *how* that could have taken place almost without even a murmur, never mind a protest. It is even more difficult to imagine *why* it happened. Was it merely a lack of resources? Was it a lack of places in residential child care or foster care? Or was it rather that the skilled persons were not available within residential child care or foster care to cope with older children, especially if they displayed signs of disturbance?

I suggest this happened, not because it was planned, but precisely the opposite — because it wasn't.

BUT NO REFORM
While new developments have taken place in the 1970s and 1980s, there has been no major, comprehensive reform or planning of our children's legislation and services. Changes have taken place on an incremental and *ad hoc* basis and piecemeal services were developed, with little or no critical evaluation of the operation. As the former Minister for Health, Mr Barry Desmond admitted:

> . . . many of these policies and services were based more on an electoral political expediency than an objective social need. All political parties

67

fell into this trap and once in a trap — what we have we hold.

(Address given at Trinity College Dublin in 1985)

WHERE HAVE THEY GONE?

But where are all these older children one may ask? Are they safe in their own homes? There are unfortunately many sad indications that they are not.

For one thing, public attention was drawn to the problem in the 1970s and 1980s with the debate about the need for places such as Loughan House and Spike Island (for young offenders). While this may have had more to do with the protection of the public and property rather than reform of services, it did draw attention to a group of young people who needed help.

Attention has been drawn to these older children also by community-based social workers and youth workers, who find it virtually impossible to get a residential place or a place of safety for children over the age of fourteen years who may need it. The state often intervenes only when the child falls foul of the law.

We know that the numbers who are under the care of the probation service, on juvenile liaison schemes, have increased dramatically over the past ten years. While we cannot prove that there is a direct correlation between the large numbers who appear in court and the lack of residential and other facilities, we do know from our experience in Focus-Point of many young people who have ended up in trouble because we could not find any form of residential care when they needed it.

Above all, attention has been drawn to homeless children and young people by the existence of numerous voluntary bodies outside the mainstream of child-care services, responding to the needs of many young people who are not receiving the type of care and protection from the state which they require. Some of these are: Los Angeles, Hope, St Vincent's Trust, Edel House, Don Bosco's, Tagaste, Hesed, Whitworth Road, Buckingham Street, Focus-Point, St Anne's Gloucester Street, Arrupe Society and Sherrard House.

These voluntary bodies provide a wide range of services for these young people who find themselves now classified as 'young homeless'. These agencies and groups are doing so with little or no statutory funding which leaves them with little influence, power or permanence to achieve anything more than a holding operation.

68

HOW MANY?
The next question people may ask is how many homeless children and young people are there in Ireland? The first answer to that is we simply do not know! We do not have any statistics with regard to the number of young people for whom the Department of Health and health boards could not provide suitable care and protection.

Random surveys carried out over a given week or month, such as the one carried out by the Eastern Health Board in Dublin in 1986, cannot disclose to us the numbers of young people and children who are out-of-home or homeless.

The experience of those of us in the voluntary agencies shows that the numbers of young homeless people is far greater than statutory bodies are prepared to acknowledge and far greater than we ourselves anticipated.

We cannot claim to have done comprehensive research on the nature and extent of youth homelessness in the whole of Ireland, but we do have valid data which gives a good indication of young homeless people in Dublin, Cork and some information on Galway. Again, this is not the result of a one-night survey or a one-month survey, but data collected over a year or more by different voluntary organisations.

In 1984 Hope hostel provided emergency and short-term accommodation for 125 boys and young men between the ages of twelve and twenty years. It said that some 38 of these young people had been sleeping out away from home for over one month before they entered the hostel.

In 1986 the report produced by an *ad hoc* group of youth, community and social workers from voluntary organisations established that 328 young people, 244 male and eighty-four female under twenty-five years were not being catered for by the existing mainstream services.

Again in 1986, Sherrard House provided emergency accommodation both short-term and long-term for 97 girls and young women between the ages of eleven and twenty-one years.

In the same year, 1986, the Don Bosco hostel had refused 30 young people because of lack of bed space. Most of these young people were between the ages of thirteen and sixteen years.

Galway Youth Services in 1987 are in contact with 25 young homeless people under eighteen years of age who are squatting or sleeping rough

69

in the city. They also believe it to be a growing problem in Galway.

In 1985, Edel House in Cork catered for forty-seven girls and young women between the ages of sixteen and twenty-five years. There is no emergency accommodation for young men or boys in Cork city in 1987.

Focus-Point's combined services of twenty-four-hour telephone help-line, information, advice and outreach streetwork has been in contact with 256 young people, 142 male and 114 female, all under eighteen years of age, between September 1985 and January 1987. During the same period, we contacted a further 180 young people aged between eighteen and twenty years. The total number of contacts of under-twenty-year-olds in Focus-Point was 436. While this is not a comprehensive piece of research, it does show clearly that there is a very large group of young people who are in need of help and who are not being catered for by the statutory agency.

You may well ask if that is the case, why don't we, the public, see them in the morning on our way to work or late at night? The very simple answer to that is that homeless young people are well aware of the stigma and prejudice attached to the term 'homeless' and they are unwilling to declare themselves as such. They appear no different from any other children or young people. Young people hide themselves for other reasons too: many of them live in fear of the police, drug pushers, criminals and pimps.

WHAT ARE THEIR PROBLEMS?
When Focus-Point came in contact with all these young people they had accommodation problems: they were either sleeping rough, dossing out, living with different friends and acquaintances, living in squats or moving in and out of hostels. They were all unemployed. Two hundred and fifty-six were under eighteen years and not entitled to social welfare, the other 180 had difficulty in claiming social welfare, because they had no fixed address.

Many had personal difficulties, such as relationship problems with their parents or families. Some had left home because of violence, sexual abuse, incest. Many had stayed at some stage in residential care. Some had developed behaviour problems since they left their home or residential care, and had become involved in drug or alcohol dependency or in crime or prostitution. Some continued to have close links with their family, but most of them had broken away from their family, and all were experiencing loneliness and isolation.

70

**CASE STUDIES: HOW PEOPLE SURVIVE AND HOW THE SYSTEM FAILS THEM**
The following stories illustrate how some of the people that we have met
in Focus-Point survive, and how the existing services respond or fail to
respond.

JIMMY'S STORY
Jimmy is known to us in Focus-Point. He is an attractive sixteen-year-old;
however, his appearance masks a very lonely and sad adolescent. He is one
of three boys in a family. His parents appear caring, but they are rigid in their
expectations of Jimmy and compare him with his brothers, who are more
successful and competitive. Communication is really poor between Jimmy
and his parents. He left home at the end of 1985 and he has been staying out
and away from home since then. When the outreach team came in contact
with him in January 1986 he had been sleeping rough, dossing with acquaintances and squatting. He claims that to survive he had had to become involved
in prostitution. This meant having casual relationships with older men for
short periods. They not only provided him with pocket money to spend on
clothes and other things, but also provided him with what he would describe
as 'a form of protection'.

HOW THE SYSTEM HAS FAILED JIMMY
Jimmy's situation illustrates many points about our current provision for
young people. For Jimmy and his family there were obviously serious problems at a very young age. Jimmy also had problems at school, from which
he was frequently absent and which he left at the age of fourteen and a
half. Yet, neither Jimmy, his parents, nor his school, for whatever reason,
sought professional help from the community-care social-work services.
*Why*? They knew there was a social worker in the health centre but they
were unaware that she could help them with Jimmy.

Once Jimmy became unattached and out of home the statutory services were
even more remote. While he is on the streets he is prey to and becomes
involved in prostitution and drug abuse. Jimmy is hard to keep in contact
with as he has no regular place where he lives — he moves about regularly.
As he is over sixteen years of age, there is no legal provision for his care and
protection. On the other hand, as he is under eighteen years he is not entitled
to social welfare payments or local authority housing. He went once to the
welfare officer but refused to return because of all the questions he was
asked. If the state does not intervene, he is likely to be prosecuted for illegal
drug abuse or prostitution.

The services Jimmy needs now in relation to his family, residential care
accommodation, training, work, activities are simply not available or accessible

to him. His only contact other than those on the streets is the outreach service of Focus-Point.

ANDY'S STORY

Andy was placed in care at the age of four. He was at risk of abuse because of serious family difficulties. He is mildly mentally handicapped. He was reared in care until he was fourteen, when he was discharged from care and returned to his parents, who by this time had separated. Since then (two years ago) he has lived intermittently with either one of his parents.

Our outreach service came in contact with him in November 1985, about six months after he had left care. At that time he was sleeping rough. Since then he has spent some time with his mother or father or sleeping rough. Most of the time he has been sleeping out because of difficulties with his parents. Between March and October of 1986 Focus-Point placed him in bed-and-breakfast accommodation on over *twenty occasions* when he refused to go home to his parents or they were unwilling to have him, and the health board was unable to find accommodation for him. On most occasions the health board paid for the bed and breakfast.

The health board social worker who works with him acknowledges that he is a difficult and demanding adolescent. His family does not have the resources to provide the care that he requires. He needs a more specialised alternative care, which is unavailable to him; he is now approaching sixteen years of age and the health board will no longer be legally responsible for him. The planned alternative residential placement has failed to materialise. This vulnerable youth has become streetwise, he knows how to get food and accommodation from different agencies in the city. Once he is out on the streets his whole physical and emotional well-being deteriorates rapidly. His real needs for care, protection, training, security, are not being addressed.

HOW THE SYSTEM HAS FAILED ANDY

Andy's situation illustrates many deficiencies in our existing provision: he was in residential care from the age of four years and was discharged ten years later to his family who were not adequately prepared for him and hadn't the resources to provide for him.

Since he has been in care he has stayed in an emergency short-term hostel, he has been in an assessment centre, he has stayed in bed and breakfasts, he has stayed with friends and strangers who take pity on him, he has stayed in presbyteries, garda stations, in hostels for older men, and he has slept out frequently. He has been in touch with a wide range of services: community care, short-term hostel, assessment centre, gardaí, numerous voluntary bodies, training workshop; yet none of these agencies, either singly or combined, can provide for him.

AILEEN'S STORY
Aileen, originally from Dublin, was put into care at the age of four, along with her two sisters. Her mother came to see them on Sundays and sometimes took them out for a picnic. Aileen used to live to see her mother at weekends. Sometimes her mother didn't turn up and this used to upset Aileen terribly.

> When she didn't come, I'd just sit in my room and cry — I wouldn't talk to anyone for days after . . .

> . . . I ran away from the orphanage a few times with one of my sisters. I was about eleven at that time. Once we made our way to Wicklow. The gardaí found us and brought us back though . . .

> When I was thirteen I was sent back home to live with my mother. Everything went fine for a few weeks and then all hell broke loose. Often after that she'd throw tantrums and often I'd run away. One day I just couldn't stand it any more. I talked with my social worker who was the only one I trusted at the time. She really cared about me. I said I needed to get out. She couldn't find anywhere for me to go. The orphanage wouldn't take me back.

Aileen was thirteen years old then. Because the social worker couldn't find residential care for Aileen she had to refer her to a hostel for homeless girls in the city. Sometimes her mother would come up and take her home, but Aileen only ran away each time. She spent two years going from place to place, her mother's, the hostel, staying with people she'd meet. Sometimes when she was barred from the hostel for aggressive behaviour she'd sleep out on the streets. Aileen used to write to her social worker but never got any reply. This was a real blow to her as the social worker was really her only contact with a helping adult. During her stay in the hostel Aileen attended a child guidance clinic.

After those two years Aileen found a flat with other friends who were staying in the hostel. The flat worked out well — the girls had their independence but had support from each other as well. None of them had much contact with their families. Aileen lived with her friends for one and a half years but was suddenly left alone when one friend left for England and the other got married.

73

. . . I started drinking a lot after a while. I had no contact with anyone hardly. I couldn't live on my own. I tried to commit suicide for the first time then — I cut both my wrists.

Aileen found herself out on the streets drinking heavily. It was at this stage that Focus-Point met her. The agency helped her to find a flat, but she was unable to cope between her drink problem, non-payment of rent, depression and inability to live with herself. Over a period of twelve months Aileen has had seven different bed-sits. She has also spent three periods in psychiatric hospitals, four periods in alcohol treatment centres, one in prison, three periods in hostels, a few nights in bed-and-breakfast accommodation and numerous nights sleeping rough on the streets.

She managed to get a place on a community workshop scheme. Her allowance was £29.50 a week. Although she was homeless, no accommodation allowance was given to her. During the training course she had to go to the welfare officer each week to obtain supplementary rent allowance. When calculated, her total weekly income was less than what she would have received from supplementary welfare allowance.

Aileen has been *seen as* an alcoholic, a mental case, an outpatient, a homeless girl, an AnCO trainee, a ward of court, a criminal, a welfare recipient.

Aileen has been *treated for* psychiatric illness, addiction problems, suicide tendency, criminal activity, homelessness.

In short, Aileen has been *seen by* psychiatrists, doctors, welfare officers, child-care guidance counsellors, social workers, specialised counsellors, gardaí, probation officers, tutors, nuns and priests. None of these, either individually or collectively, could help Aileen out of her situation.

She is now eighteen years old. A victim of a family disaster, she has spent five years homeless. She has an addiction problem, she suffers from severe depression, she is poor, her health is very bad, she has few, if any, real friends. Yet Aileen is an intelligent, loving and talented person.


HOW THE SYSTEM HAS FAILED AILEEN
Through Aileen's story are demonstrated a number of deficiencies in our child-care services:

When Aileen returned from child care to her mother's home there was no follow-up support or care for either herself or her mother. This might have prevented a worsening of the home situation or ensured that Aileen had alternative care and accommodation.

When she left home at the age of thirteen years no residential care could be found for her.

The only significant person in Aileen's life, her social worker, dropped her when she left the locality.

With the lack of support and accommodation Aileen developed a severe drink problem.

Aileen could cope in a flat once she had the support of friends — she couldn't live on her own with no support.

Aileen held a place on an AnCO training scheme while she was homeless. She received the minimum allowance of £29.50 — less than the supplementary welfare allowance. She had no accommodation allowance, which is available to trainees on other courses in the city. This is in contrast with young people who have to leave home to take part in other AnCO courses.

At no stage during her homelessness was there any comprehensive attempt to help her. Individual symptoms were treated in isolation, eg alcoholism, aggression, depression etc.

Aileen's case is not unusual. A series of factors have worked against her for which she is paying dearly.

MARY'S STORY
Mary is fourteen years of age and is still at school. She is one of a family of five children. Since the age of twelve Mary has been sexually abused by her father at home. A year ago Mary courageously confided in her mother who took her to a child-guidance clinic. Mary attended the clinic regularly over the year. Residential care was not available. After another threatening and terrifying period at home, she spent time in a psychiatric centre. She then again returned home. The relationship still continues with her father. Mary has attempted suicide and mutilated herself on several occasions. She has been truanting from school and often at night sleeps rough out in the city. Mary experiences long periods of depression.

HOW THE SYSTEM HAS FAILED MARY
Mary now desperately wants to leave home and find a place of safety so that she can keep up a relationship with the other family members, particularly

her mother. Mary's mother would like her to be placed in a place of safety, but despite collaborated efforts of community care, social workers, teachers, child-guidance counsellors, psychiatrists, doctors, neighbours and priests, all have been unable to find a suitable place for her.

The reason for their failure is simply that there is no suitable therapeutic residential centre or place of safety for Mary and many others like her, who need safety, security, care, protection, warmth and structure.


**LEGISLATION AND SERVICES URGENTLY NEEDED**
These four cases highlight serious deficiencies in our current legislation, policies and services relating to young people out-of-home.

LEGISLATION
Young people *aged sixteen to eighteen* years and out-of-home are a particularly vulnerable group: there is no legal obligation on the state to provide

- care and protection — they are too old for child-care and too young for income assistance
- income maintenance within or outside the family
- local authority housing

Young homeless children *under sixteen* years are denied their right of legal care and protection under our existing children's legislation. The state is unable or unwilling to intervene when boys and girls are involved in prostitution or are being sexually abused at home.

SERVICES, SUPPORT AND CARE
There are certain obvious identifiable needs in the area of services, support and care which could prevent youth homelessness, intervene in crisis situations and provide on-going care for children and young people out-of-home and families with special needs.

- *Information* Families who are having difficulties with their children should know where to go to look for help.
- *Family support services* which would enable families get through various crises in their lives are needed. These should act preventatively, so that young people and children could be maintained in the community.
- *Accessibility to services* The existing statutory services are in the main

76

remote and inaccessible to young people. Some are remote geographically, others are remote culturally.

- *Therapeutic care* There is a need for specialised therapeutic care for the more disturbed and scared children and adolescents.

- *Variety of community-based centres* There is a need for a wide range of services at the community level in areas where there is a high incidence of homeless children and young people — such as outreach work, drop-in centres, structured youth clubs, emergency accommodation provision, family support services.

- *Adequate after-care services* are needed for young people who have been reared in care to reintegrate them back into their families and communities. Young people who have been in care form a significant group of the homeless population.

- *Adequate supportive services for young people out-of-home*, which will help them to return home is possible, or if not, to find alternative care and accommodation, are needed. Without proper supportive services the young person is likely to develop other problems such as alcohol abuse or drug addiction, or become involved in prostitution and crime and become increasingly alienated from the family and other adults.

- *Alternative suitable accommodation for young people out-of-home* There is a need for more emergency accommodation, short-term hostels, short-term care, long-term hostels and social housing.

- *Assessment and child guidance* There is a need for more assessment centres and child-guidance clinics in the cities and around the country.

- *Development of residential and foster care* for children and young people over twelve years who cannot live at home is required.

- *Supportive training centres* There is a need for special income arrangements for young people out-of-home who participate in training programmes. Young homeless people under eighteen years in AnCO community work-shop training courses only receive minimum allowances — £29.50, less than supplementary welfare allowance — with no accommodation allowance. This is in marked contrast to the accommodation allowance given to young people who have had to leave home to take part in other AnCO courses.

- *Co-ordination and integrated approach* There is a very unintegrated service response to young people out-of-home by both the statutory and voluntary organisations. A young person can be availing of help from any one of the following range of services: Eastern Health Board; social

77

work and community welfare service; AnCO training; gardaí, hostels, day centres, residential centres, assessment centres, voluntary organisations, housing department, probation welfare service, prison service, training centres, youth services, juvenile liaison service. Any of these singly or together are often unable to meet their wide-ranging needs at any one time.

- There is a lack of communication between statutory agencies working with young people and between voluntary organisations and statutory agencies.

- There is a need for formal structure involving the statutory agencies and voluntary agencies together in planning and delivering services for the young homeless.

**QUESTIONS TO ADDRESS**

It seems to me that there is a direct parallel with what happened in the economic sphere in Ireland in the 1960s and 1970s and what happened to young homeless people in Ireland in those decades. It was commonly believed in the 1960s that everyone would benefit in the economic boom and in the rising tide all boats would rise. Of course now we know that this did not happen, but it wasn't until the 1971 Poverty Conference in Kilkenny that we were reminded that 25 per cent of our population were living below the poverty line. That reminder to the nation did not lead to an immediate redistribution of resources or herald a new social order. In fact, it was met with a mixed reaction ranging from shock to scepticism about poverty and justice, but it started a debate which still goes on and has brought only some changes.

Similarly in the child-care field it was commonly believed that all our children would benefit from changes in the children's services in the 1970s and 1980s and in spite of reminders from the voluntary sector that young people were falling through the cracks in the services, it took the closure of Hope hostel * in 1986 to call attention to young homeless people. But as in the case of poverty, the closure of Hope did not herald a new era in the children's services.

But what the closure of Hope hostel did was to start a debate on youth homelessness which still goes on and must go on. It raises questions and must continue to raise questions which must be addressed and answered; about

*Hope hostel was the only emergency and short-term hostel for boys in Dublin and was closed in April 1986.

how its closure was responded to by the Health Board, the Department of Health and the Minister for Health. What does it tell us, if anything, about their knowledge, understanding and commitment to young people who are homeless and extremely vulnerable? How, for example, was it possible to find money overnight for Loughan House and Spike Island when it took nine months to find the funds and agreement to replace Hope hostel? While unreservedly welcoming the establishment of Percy Place* as a short-term hostel and the fact that it is properly funded, one would have to ask how was it possible to increase funding for the hostel four-fold when people were led to understand that there was no funding available? Of course a voluntary hostel should be established with proper facilities and a stable source of funding, but questions must be asked about how decisions are made? Was the response to Hope hostel nine months later another example of political expediency rather than an objective response to need?

Again, the recruitment of more social workers to work with young homeless people is to be welcomed, but is it too much to expect discussions to take place between statutory departments and voluntary bodies who are already employing social workers in that field before these decisions are made?

These are all questions about needs and resources but they are also questions about strategy and planning in relation to the structure and delivery of our services. They are fundamental questions about trust, respect and co-operation. Above all, they are questions about power and control. These questions must be addressed *now*; otherwise, we will continue to make an *ad hoc* piecemeal and fragmented response to the situation.

What about the voluntary agencies working with young people who are called 'homeless'? Are we prepared to go on providing a separate service inadequately funded for some of our most hurt and vulnerable young people, who are no different to those being cared for in the mainstream services except that the services cannot care for them or have failed them? We should remember that children who are being cared for within the mainstream services are as much homeless and out-of-home as those who are sleeping out or squatting, or dossing or staying in hostels.

Are we going to collude with a society that likes to see homeless people as different? The popular perception of homeless people is that they are smelly, dirty, different, outcasts, no good. That perception affects people's attitudes,

*Percy Place was opened as an emergency short-term hostel in Dublin in December 1986.

79

which in turn affect their response. If our response is to provide a separate service with inadequate funding and no security, then we are confirming society's image of the homeless person: that they are different and as such, should be treated separately; that they don't deserve to be treated with the dignity and respect which all our children deserve.

Homelessness and the lack of basic human needs is not only a shocking reality but a terrible indictment on all of us. We all unwittingly participate in that system of injustice whether it is in Bombay, Guatemala, Peru, Calcutta, New York or Dublin. We must accept our responsibility for condemning hundreds of millions of people to the ravages of hunger, disease and infection.

The fact that Ireland has given £25,000 towards relief of homelessness in the Third World in 1987 does not relieve us of our responsibility. Neither should we be comforted by the fact that we haven't got the type of homelessness there is in the Third World. It is believed that only in a society which is well off can people value and protect their children. Yet, we have in the midst of great affluence, a desperate poverty. Unequal distribution of wealth has promoted misery and division in the lives of many people. Fragmentation in our society has led to new kinds of pressures which create conflict in society, communities and families. The dominating values of affluence often divide homes and create homelessness. So it is in this context that we must address the problems and needs of all our children: the solutions to these touch the very basis of our socio-economic and political structures.

It is not without good reason that the United Nations has designated 1987 as the International Year of Shelter for the Homeless, and if we are not prepared to accept the responsibility for the reality that exists, it is not only a tragedy but a crime against billions of children and young people around the world.

by Stanislaus Kennedy RSC

I would like to acknowledge the help given to me by the people of Focus-Point in preparing this paper. S.K.

1. J. Robins, *The Lost Children*, Institute of Public Administration, Dublin 1980.
2. *Report on the Reformatory and Industrial Schools System*, Dublin Stationery Office 1969.
3. *Ibid.*
4. *Ibid.*
5. *Children in Care*, Department of Health, Dublin 1983.

Photographs by kind permission of Rachel Collier. Royal Society of Antiquaries of Ireland, and UNICEF (William Hetzer, Ray Witlin, Claudio Edinger and Bernard P. Wolff).

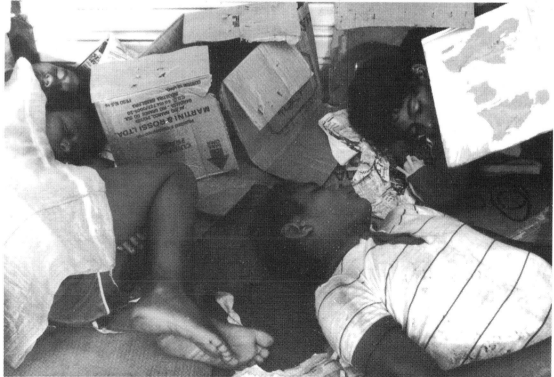

# Care and Protection of the Young Out-of-Home

## Care and Protection for Young People Out-of-Home: An Overview

### ROLE OF DEPARTMENT OF HEALTH

The Ad Hoc Committee on the Homeless, which reported in 1984, referred to the problem of homeless children, ie persons under eighteen years of age. The committee, which was representative of the Departments of Health, Social Welfare and the Environment together with the local authorities and the health boards, considered that the accommodation and other needs of homeless children could best be met by health boards. This recommendation was endorsed in the government's national youth policy — *In Partnership with Youth* — published in 1985. The Housing (Miscellaneous Provisions) Bill, 1985 did not make specific provision for persons under eighteen years of age and it is generally accepted that, with some few exceptions, responsibility for the care and protection of young people out-of-home is more appropriate to health boards than to local authorities.

### DEPARTMENT'S POLICY IN RELATION TO YOUNG PEOPLE OUT-OF-HOME

The general policy of the Department of Health is that every child should be brought up in his or her own family. So, the main thrust and focus of future developments will be to provide a range of family support services which will prevent or diminish to the greatest extent possible the risk of children leaving home or being placed in care. This important policy objective was incorporated in the Children (Care and Protection) Bill 1985.

### PREVENTATIVE SERVICES

In a sense a child may be said to be homeless long before he or she leaves the shelter of his or her home. A home means more than a roof over one's head: it also means love and acceptance and unity. Where these are absent there is no home. The act of leaving home is merely the final stage for some young people who have had to endure a wretched family life.

Some children may be considered to be at risk from infancy in homes where there is discord, deprivation or inadequate parenting. Front-line staff working with such families need to be sensitive to a range of indicative factors, such as truancy, disturbed behaviour or experimentation with alcohol in children, as well as other features ranging from the more obvious problems

81

associated with low income, such as inadequate housing, single parents, to the less conspicuous threats, such as suspected violence or abuse.

There is a need, therefore, for a much greater range of social and educational services at the preventative level.

This is the crucial stage at which families and children can be supported in achieving positive lifestyles. Interventions will need to range from advice on family planning to innovative educational projects for parents and children alike. Some services, although limited in scope, are already in place, for example day-care centres, family resource units, neighbourhood youth projects.

The recently published consultative statement on health policy — *Health — The Wider Dimensions* — refers to the wider role of the health services in relation to a range of social problems. It points out that current social trends would suggest that the demand for such services is likely to grow in future years and recommends that personal social services should be given a stronger identity at national and local levels. I myself would strongly favour a rigorous preventative policy to cover a wide spectrum of family problems.

I would be doubtful, however, whether in the present political and economic climate it will be possible to make improvements as rapidly as we would like. The cost of our present acute hospital services, in particular, hangs like a mill-stone around the neck of the health services and makes it very difficult to bring about quickly a shift in emphasis from institutional to community-based services. Nevertheless, there is movement in that direction.

**NUMBERS OF HOMELESS CHILDREN**
Wherever there is one child who has temporarily or permanently left home there is a need for a response. I must, however, question whether the levels of child homelessness which are sometimes quoted are accurate. We may, in fact, need to draw a distinction between children who are homeless and children who are out-of-home. I would suggest that children are often out-of-home before they become finally homeless, and that children out-of-home are a more common phenomenon.

A random survey might disclose quite a number of young people who could be described as out-of-home on any given night, especially in the greater Dublin area. Such children may have left home temporarily but have a very real prospect of reconciliation if they are offered appropriate assistance.

The intervention strategies could range from individual counselling to temporary fostering or crisis hostel placement.

The aim of the intervention must always be the early return of the child to his or her family wherever this is possible. This, of course, may involve long and intensive family support. I would reject the labelling of such a child as homeless since this label can create its own stigma and reduce the role of the family. Homeless children, as I interpret it, are the group who may have been availing of residential, health and educational services on a long-term basis and have lost contact with their families. Where possible, fostering may prove an appropriate response to their dilemma but it would have to be fostering of a very specialised nature. With the possibility of future legislative developments allowing legitimate children to be adopted, adoption should become another alternative.

The possibility of either arrangement within the child's extended family might also be worthy of consideration.

**PERCY PLACE HOSTEL AND ASSOCIATED EASTERN HEALTH BOARD SOCIAL WORK SERVICE**
A new service for homeless children was opened at Percy Place, Dublin, at the end of last year. The hostel, which can cater for up to ten boys, was established following the report of a task force convened by the former Minister for Health. The Percy Place service, which is being run under the auspices of the Catholic Social Service Conference, is providing more than just shelter. The intention is that while young people are living in the hostel they will be helped to deal with the problems which caused their predicament. Counselling, social work and training services will be made available as required.

The maximum stay is envisaged as twelve weeks, after which residents are helped to return home, to seek an independent life or to settle into a more long-term supportive service. The task force, in making its recommendations to the minister, was unanimously of the view that the hostel should have associated with it support services reaching out into the community and into the root cause of why the young people ended up on the street. Consequently, the Eastern Health Board was provided with resources to recruit five additional social workers who will be community-based but will liaise with the hostel service.

These new appointees will, it is hoped, also have contact with young people at risk and those on the verge of leaving home. They will have an especially valuable role in establishing contact with young people out-of-home who may be staying with friends, in squats or other temporary forms of accommodation.

The task force, in considering the question of homeless children in Dublin, met with and had before it a number of reports from individuals and groups concerned with the problem. Amongst these groups were the National Campaign for the Homeless and the Campaign Group for Homeless Youth. A major cause for hope in the area of homelessness is the wide number of organisations involved with homeless persons at present.

## CONCLUSION
I would like to make a suggestion by way of conclusion. Eleven different organisations involved with the homeless came together last year and produced a comprehensive report on care and accommodation for young people at risk or homeless in Dublin. One of the issues raised in the report was the lack of co-ordination in services. One might ask whether at least some scarce resources and energies are being dissipated by this lack of cohesion.

I urge all voluntary and statutory agencies to work very closely in planning and delivering services. This International Year of Shelter for the Homeless is a particularly appropriate time in which to consider the possibilities that exist for a fully co-ordinated approach to the care and protection of children out-of-home.

by Dr Joseph Robins

# Residential Care for Young People Out-of-Home

Residential care is generally thought of as children's homes and hostels pro- vided under the direction of the community care programmes of the health boards, usually by voluntary or religious bodies. However, residential care is also provided by the mental handicap services, under the probation and welfare services of the Department of Justice and under special education services. Young people also receive 'residential care' of a sort for long periods in hospitals, treatment units and prison services.

## INSTITUTIONAL v COMMUNITY CARE
In recent years, there have been rapid changes in society, attitudes to child- rearing and degrees of personal responsibility for relationships and actions. It is not long since it was quite acceptable for those who were dependent or non-conforming to the mores or behaviour accepted as normal to be 'looked

after' in large institutions — schools, children's homes, hostels, county homes, hospitals, prisons. By their nature, such institutions were authoritarian and could not treat people individually according to their needs, personal and individual relationships and their different and individual stages of development. Following the Kennedy Report in Ireland (1970), such defects were recognised and for practical, social and philosophical reasons there has been a swing towards care within individuals' own communities, or, where necessary, providing a new community. This is often seen as a cheaper option, but if it were properly supported, it is doubtful if it actually would be a less expensive way to look after people. In any case, if this is the direction services are to go in, it should be because it is better for the individual and better for the community, not because it is believed to be cheaper.

## THE STATE AND THE VOLUNTARY SECTOR

Children's bills have recently been introduced, addressing much-needed reforms, most of which will cost more money. The more the state acknowledges needs, the more it creates an expectation that it can provide the necessary money, but it is not at all clear that this money can in fact be provided. The provision of care by large voluntary or religious bodies is diminishing, and increased responsibility is being thrust onto the statutory services, but there is a frightening lack of commonly accepted policy and co-operation among the various organisations. Much of this confusion is expressed in financial terms: it is not clear what services are required and what services the state is expected to provide and to fund.

There are considerable skills, goodwill, energy and enthusiasm in the state organisations involved in services for children, but much of this energy is siphoned off into clarifying areas of responsibility, finding out who does what, who needs what, and trying to create systems for co-operation and co-ordination of services. Yet when one organisation responds to a need, the others feel less responsible, and it is almost a matter of chance which type of service a child receives: for instance, a child who enters the mental handicap section or the justice section will receive the service they can offer rather than the service he or she needs.

It is not only statutory services that work in isolation: too many voluntary bodies also appear to have difficulty in working with each other in a complementary way. Many organisations appear to assume that they can only provide what they can control, perhaps indicating a basic lack of confidence in each other. Many voluntary organisations are dependent on statutory bodies for funds and have difficulty in negotiating for these funds. Since the voluntary bodies are in competition with each other for funds, they tend to negotiate for the lowest amounts they can manage on, and do not include back-up staff, management and support services in their budgets. This inevitably results in an inadequate service.

## MEETING STREETWISE CHILDREN'S SPECIAL NEEDS
We can assume that streetwise young people who are in need of residential care have had at worst damaging and at best confusing experiences and relationships, at a time when they are moving from the social status and relationships of childhood to those of adulthood. They are at an age when young people are living with or are expected to live with their families, and the extra difficulties, insecurities and disruptions in their relationships and development may be reflected in their behaviour and ability to develop satisfactory relationships. If their adjustments and behaviour were satisfactory, they would be unlikely to come to the notice of providers of special services in the first place. We do not have, nor do we need services for those who are easy.

It is simplistic to think that the needs of, let's say, thirty fourteen-to-eighteen-year-old boys for hostel care can be met by four hostels with eight places each. It may not be possible, for instance, to place a disruptive boy in a hostel that already has disruptive children and needs more easily managed children to achieve a balance; or a particular boy may need services such as work or day-time activities which the hostel that has a bed free cannot provide. What is needed is not just places in hostels, but services tailored to the needs of the individual young person, and a method of assessing what those needs are. It is likely that in the future we will need a different balance of residential provision, community-based services, family placements, sheltered accommodation.

The assessment centres and short-term hostels do at present assess needs, but they have to accept that what is needed is often not available. This means not only that the individual does not get what he or she needs, but also the short-term provision becomes long- or medium-term. This results in insecurity for the person concerned, a rejection of an opportunity to settle and discouragement for the staff. We need assessment meetings where the representatives have access to several services to see how together they can provide a package of services tailored to the individual's needs.

## WHAT RESIDENTIAL UNITS SHOULD OFFER
On the whole it is now accepted that residential homes and hostels should have a homely atmosphere and the opportunity for close relationships between the staff and young people. There should be an emphasis also on maintaining links as far as possible with parents, siblings and extended family. Whether these produce 'satisfactory' relationships or not, the young person derives his

86

or her sense of identity largely from his or her family and it needs to be acknowledged. It is important also that residential units should be part of a range of services, and half-way or sheltered accommodation should be available with contact and support from staff for young people who are approaching greater independence.

This sort of service makes considerable demands on the skills, energy, flexibility, understanding and resourcefulness of staff, and this means that staff need training, encouragement and back-up, with time off for relief and study. This will require greater resources of staff. There is no shortage of committed and energetic people capable of providing care — what is missing is the organisational will, support and money to provide them with what they need to carry out the work.

**A CENTRAL BODY**
What is needed to tackle the problems of the system is one body with the power and commitment to co-ordinate the services of all the providers, both statutory and voluntary. Energy that is at present being directed into competing with other bodies for finance and approval should be redirected towards creative co-operation, and those in need should be seen as individuals rather than categorised into types. It is not only more efficient but also more responsible to have a central focus for all services. Unless there is an overall framework within which all the services to young people can work, young people will continue to become streetwise and all the best efforts of the short-term or assessment services will be wasted, for if the young person has nowhere suitable to go he or she will return to the situation they were already in, even more discouraged and disillusioned.

by Laetitia Lefroy

# Emergency and Short Term Accommodation for Young Homeless People

The provision of emergency and short-term accommodation is arguably the most important and urgent response required to the problem of homelessness amongst young people after they have left home. This is so for two reasons.

First, for the majority of young people who leave home, homelessness is a temporary phenomenon. Tension at home, difficulty in relating to one or both parents, a difficulty in coping with an alcoholic parent or similar factors may lead a young person to seek a solution to the problem by 'escaping' from it. The failure to provide *immediate* help and support to such young people exposes some of them unnecessarily to the risk of permanent homelessness. If the problem with the family is allowed to go untouched for any length of time, the alienation of the young person from their family, or the alienation of the parents from the young person, may increase to the point where it becomes impossible for the young person to return home.

Secondly, the longer a young person remains on the streets, the more difficult it is for him or her to return to a dependency status, either at home or in a hostel. On the streets, a young person quickly experiences a form of independence, fending for him/herself, nobody telling them what to do, being in apparent control of their own decisions. A lengthy experience of this sort may make a return to the dependency of a normal twelve- or thirteen-year-old very difficult. Hence the provision of an adequate emergency and short-term service to young homeless people is a high priority. The failure to spend money on such a service will certainly entail much higher costs in the long term, as more residential accommodation will be required for some young people who might otherwise have been enabled to return home and an unnecessary increase in the social and mental problems that homelessness create becomes inevitable.

**EMERGENCY AND SHORT-TERM ACCOMMODATION**

A distinction has to be made between *emergency* accommodation, strictly speaking, and *short-term* accommodation. Often both of these are condensed into one service, not altogether satisfactorily.

*Emergency accommodation* is designed to cater for the immediate need for shelter for a young person who has left home and has nowhere to stay. Access is guaranteed, no interviews are required. The rationale for such a shelter is that each person is entitled to food and shelter as a basic right. Frequently, the staff will be in a position to help the young person make decisions about his/her future without too much difficulty.

However, in other cases a longer or shorter period of assessment may be required. A *short-term accommodation* service provides a young person with a longer period — perhaps up to three months — in which they can find space to reflect on their future. It would provide experienced counsellors to help this process and may seek the help of more professional assessments (eg psychiatric, psychological). It would provide a breathing space in which work with the family could be undertaken. During this period of assessment, the long-term accommodation options would be discussed and planned for.

In any such discussions, the young person him/herself would have a major say. Any decision which is going to be successful must be the decision of the young person him/herself.

RECENT HISTORY

The recent history of emergency and short-term accommodation in this country makes rather pathetic reading. In April 1986, Hope hostel, the only emergency accommodation for young homeless people in Ireland, closed for lack of funds. An offer of £60,000 from the Eastern Health Board was clearly insufficient to run an efficient service without adding to an already heavy debt problem. It was insisted that there was simply no further money available given the state of public finances. The Eastern Health Board promised that an even better service would be established to replace it. However, as the months passed, no such service appeared. Voluntary bodies noticed a significant increase in the number of young homeless people coming to them. The Eastern Health Board and the Department of Health were at loggerheads over who should fund the service. Responsibility for the service belonged to the Eastern Health Board but they were facing cut-backs in funding from the Department of Health and did not see how they could allocate more than the £60,000 already promised to Hope. The Department of Health would not allocate extra funding to them to do so, insisting that the funding should come out of their existing budget. While they disputed where the money was going to come from many young homeless people were forced to sleep rough.

Finally, in November, the Minister for Health announced the setting-up of a task force whose job it was to get a substitute service for Hope off the ground within four weeks. He also announced that money would not be a problem.

At the end of the four-week period, the only realistic proposal before them was one from the Dublin diocese offering to start a service immediately. The cost of such a service would be over £200,000 a year. The minister had no option but to accept. It would appear that the coming of Christmas (homeless children at Christmas would be an issue the media could not ignore!) with the prospect of an election early in the new year pushed the issue of emergency accommodation to the top of the political agenda. (This is not to deny the genuine concern of individual ministers or even of the cabinet; it is simply to reflect on the transition from concern to political action.)

For almost nine months, many young homeless people lived on the streets, some became involved in crime, others in prostitution, all were damaged in some way by their experiences because Hope hostel was told in April that

89

the state did not have the money to provide more than £60,000 per year to fund an emergency and short-term service to meet the needs of young homeless people.

## LINK WITH POVERTY AND UNEMPLOYMENT

Homelessness amongst young people has, in recent years, acquired two new characteristics. First, what was once a trickle of young people leaving home has become a flood. Secondly, the age at which young people are abandoning their homes is becoming younger. Ten- and eleven-year-olds sleeping on the streets no longer astonish youth workers. Both of these developments suggest that youth homelessness cannot be seen in isolation from other aspects of Irish society and that a response to the problem must go beyond the mere provision of accommodation and services. While the causes of homelessness amongst young people are complex, the link with *unemployment* and *poverty* must be stressed. In a recent survey undertaken by an *ad hoc* group of youth and community workers, 89 per cent of young homeless people were identified as coming from seven areas, namely, Finglas, Ballymun, Ballyfermot, city centre, Dun Laoghaire, Tallaght and Coolock. The majority of these areas are characterised by high unemployment (eg Ballymun has 61 per cent unemployed). As almost 50 per cent of those unemployed are now registered as long-term unemployed, the problem of poverty is also a characteristic of these areas. It seems to me that unemployment and poverty are imposing strains on families which those families can no longer withstand. Homelessness amongst young people is simply one manifestation of these strains, alongside mental problems, increased alcoholism, increased violence and sexual abuse and so forth. These may have been families who were coping, perhaps not very well but nevertheless coping, with problems before unemployment added to their burdens. They were, in many cases, families where it was evident that long-term unemployment was going to wreak havoc. Frequently, nothing is done to help them until their problems explode and then it may often be too late.

If one takes this broader perspective and if one accepts the priority of emergency and short-term accommodation in responding to the problem *after* it happens, then it is clear that as unemployment and poverty increase, the provision of emergency services should likewise increase. In fact the opposite is more likely to happen. As the demands on social expenditure increase, the finances deemed available are spread ever more thinly and services such as emergency and short-term accommodation, far from expanding to meet a growing problem, may in fact shrink, at least relative to the total problem. While the very substantial funding made available to the service in Percy Place is very welcome (and the quality of service available is much improved) the fact is that the number of places available for emer-

90

gency and short-term accommodation for young people is now *less* than ever before.

## RESPONSES NEEDED

I would suggest here a further service which the extent of the problem today might suggest as necessary. The survey mentioned above indicates seven areas from which 89 per cent of young homeless people come. A response needs to be targeted on those areas. The response required is two-fold: first preventative work and secondly rehabilitative work.

The whole area of prevention, working with families in stress in order to reduce the likelihood of children having to leave home, is fundamental and of the highest priority in dealing with the problem of homelessness, but is not the focus of this paper.

Some disagreement exists as to whether help for young people who have already left home should be available within the locality from which they came or whether that help should be given at a central venue located in a different area. Some will argue that most young people who leave home also leave the area in which they are living; hence the response should be elsewhere, for instance in the city centre. My own experience is that, at least with older youth, many do in fact wish to remain within their home area. Hence I would argue that in each of the seven target areas there ought to be an advice and day centre which would include a service to young people who have left home. Ideally, this service would also provide a small residential unit which can provide emergency accommodation within their own area to those who wish to remain there. The advice and day centre would be part of a broader service to the whole neighbourhood, provided directly by the Eastern Health Board, but would be clearly identifiable as the first step in the provision of help to a young person who has left home. The residential unit, which would be small, could be run by a local voluntary or community group who maintain close liaison with the Eastern Health Board day service. Such a service would not replace the larger, more organised emergency and short-term service provided in a central area such as now exists in Percy Place. It would rather work alongside and in close co-operation with it.

## PROBLEMS

The Percy Place hostel has managed to avoid most of the problems I outline here, but these problems tend to arise with emergency and short-term provision generally.

First, the 'railway station' mentality. A low standard of accommodation, overcrowding, inexperienced staff and lack of facilities may be evident in emergency accommodation, because it is felt that since young people are only there a short time, such inadequacies don't really matter. However, such a service requires a level of expertise amongst the staff which is above average, not below it. The constant dealing with new youngsters and the range of problems which these youngsters present impose very considerable demands on the staff. The provision of drab, overcrowded accommodation which badly needs a coat of paint and the inadequacy of the facilities available may make the streets appear more attractive to young people.

Secondly, an emergency service can come to be seen as primarily the provision of food and accommodation. Adequate counselling, family work and the space in which to think and feel more clearly and with less confusion can come to be given a lower priority than the more evident need for food and shelter. It is to the credit of our new emergency and short-term service in Percy Place that this has been avoided.

Thirdly, the lack of adequate follow-through facilities can reduce enormously the usefulness of an emergency and short-term service. Not only can the residential aspect of the service become cluttered up with young people for whom no other placement can be found but it can quickly become a priority to try and 'get him in somewhere'. An excellent assessment service may be provided, everyone, including the young persons themselves, may be very clear as to what is needed, but it simply is not available. A very inadequate placement may be all that is available. Sometimes, particularly for the more difficult young person, no placement at all can be found.

Fourthly, the lack of co-ordination of services may present an emergency and short-term service with great difficulties. In Ireland, at present there are at least three ages at which different options become available:

Many young people leave residential care at the age of sixteen with nowhere to go and unable to cope with independent living. A significant proportion of young homeless people were previously in residential care. The provision of supportive accommodation for over-sixteens is particularly acute and *no agency or government department has responsibility for this age group*.

At eighteen, young people may find accommodation in the adult hostels in Dublin. It goes without saying, of course, that this is hopelessly unsatisfactory. Nevertheless, the adult hostels are finding young people of that age with nowhere to go and reluctantly accept them. Thus, if one approaches a government department for assistance for a residential project for this age-group, there is a tendency to downplay the need for such a service since the adult hostels already provide one!

92

And finally, at the age of twenty you may be eligible for consideration by Dublin Corporation for independent accommodation. However, there is no obligation on the corporation to house single people of this age and it appears that often the decision depends on the impression which the young person makes on the official dealing with his/her case. This lack of co-ordination ensures that services are provided piecemeal, voluntary agencies seeking funding and support are passed from one department to another and huge gaps in the provision of services are inevitable.

### A SECURE UNIT?
Emergency or short-term accommodation services encounter young people who have become used to making all their own decisions. Because they have been out on the streets for a considerable length of time and are therefore accustomed to being their own boss, or because of the failure of their parents to impose any controls, they have been running their own lives anyway.

In such a situation, any controls which are imposed will be resisted and the hostel will experience the young person as extraordinarily difficult and dis-ruptive. Great sensitivity is required to both maintain some order yet not drive the young person away as the shift back from independence to a form of dependency is extremely difficult for a young person. Here I simply raise an issue for discussion. Does the absence of any secure or semi-secure unit in which this can be accomplished impose great difficulties for existing hostels?

*In favour* of such a proposal, there are, in my experience, a small number of young people who simply cannot be served by existing hostel-type accom-modation on its own. Running away becomes the response even to mild challenges to personal behaviour. The eventual outcome for the young person is inevitably a custodial sentence in the criminal courts. *Against* such a pro-posal would be the reality that such a unit quickly becomes over-used. The tendency is that young people who are difficult to manage get referred to such a centre for the sake of the *hostel*, not the *child*. If such a unit is thought necessary, it should be closely linked to some existing short-term accommodation service, should only be used as a final resort and only for as short a period as possible.

by Peter McVerry, SJ

# Youth Services for Homeless Young Persons in Cork

The provision of shelter for homeless people is only the first step in providing for their needs. It is only through loving concern for individuals in deprived situations that the growth of a delinquent minority can be prevented, and it is for this reason that I maintain that setting up structures physically to house the homeless is not enough. Many young people who live at home, are 'at home' in name only, and it is the poverty of emotional life rather than the lack of material things that brings about a state of mind leading to delinquent behaviour. Many young people suffer the most appalling difficulties with their families, and the strained relationships may be so tragic that they are left with no alternative but to opt out and leave home. There is no doubt that remedial care at family level has to be tackled, and soon, but it is equally certain that state bodies are unwilling to admit that this need even exists. The Department of Health has the overall legal responsibility for the distribution of social services to children and young people, and co-ordination between the voluntary and statutory bodies is therefore of the utmost importance. While people are in desperate need of services, negotiation procedures take a long time to be finalised and people are neglected and the problem of homelessness gathers momentum.

**PRESENT PROVISION IN CORK**
There has been an increase in the number of day-care facilities in Cork city, mostly run by voluntary agencies. These include AnCO workshops, private enterprises for boys, neighbourhood youth schemes, youth employment projects, day services for ex-prisoners, family support centres, a rape crisis centre, the Arbour House drugs centre, the Cura service, the Simon community, Alcoholics Anonymous, the Samaritans and the St Vincent de Paul Society.

The night shelter accommodation deals only with the tip of the iceberg. Edel House was started in 1972 to cater for homeless girls, women and children and in 1985 forty-seven girls between sixteen and twenty-five availed of the facility. Of these, six spent from one to three months and four from three to six months there. Thirty per cent stayed longer than two weeks.

This highlighted the necessity for supervised transitional accommodation and so flats were provided for this age-group. Many of the young women saw moving into a flat as an immediate solution to their need for accommodation, but their lack of maturity, emotional problems, previous experiences of rejection and insecurity, made them vulnerable in private flats or bedsitters. The length of stay in these flats is envisaged as any period up to a year.

The provision of private accommodation is the next step, but before this is undertaken it first needs to be assessed very carefully. Further legislation is needed which will ensure standardisation in the private rented sector and registration of landlords is long overdue. The accommodation is in many cases grossly inadequate and unsuitable and so costly that those who depend on social benefits are left without enough to live on once they have paid the high weekly rent which may be anything from twenty to thirty-three pounds a week.

The problem of providing accommodation for girls is less serious than for boys, especially for those from twelve to eighteen years of age. Estimated figures furnished by the probation service of young people at risk totals about five hundred, of which 10 per cent are girls. The 90 per cent of boys are solvent abusers or heavy drinkers.

Hostel accommodation, such as that provided by Edel House, provides immediate shelter for homeless girls, women and children, but a hostel is no substitute for a home and should not be regarded as such: it is only a temporary facility to allow the young person or adult time to adjust and the opportunity to find permanent accommodation or to become reunited with their family. The St Vincent de Paul Society provides shelter for men, but there is a whole range of services not provided by either of these bodies.

### NEEDS OF THE MARRIED HOMELESS
In Cork at the moment husbands are tragically separated from mothers and children. During times of family stress, where relatives and friends fail, night shelters are the only facility available. The separation of husband and wife is felt keenly by the mother who needs the support of her husband, by the children who are confused and frightened, and by the father whose anger at the situation is coupled with a feeling of inadequacy and humiliation. The family should be kept together as a family but there is no service for this specific purpose.

The Housing Department will not take responsibility for childless married couples. It would be a welcome piece of legislation which would allow the Housing Department to place newly married couples on a housing list and not oblige them to wait until a baby arrives. At present, while awaiting housing accommodation they have a private flat allocated to them. The high price causes a heavy financial burden at the beginning of their married life and having to wait for an indeterminate time can be additionally frustrating.

### NEEDS OF THE SINGLE HOMELESS
There is a whole range of services needed for young people in this category — for boys who are put out of home because of membership in a gang, for girls who are pregnant, for those who have become so difficult at home that their parents cannot cope with them any longer. Then there are those who leave home of their own accord because they resent limits being set to their

95

freedom. They go to night shelters but leave them for the same reasons that they had left home — freedom to do what they like.

There are also the multiple-problem youths. These are often slow learners and because there is no specific service provision to cater for their needs, they sometimes drift into situations of co-habitation with older men.

Then there are the homeless 'gangs' of teenage drinkers, drug addicts and those whose parents want them out. The spiral continues its downward trend from conflict with the law, to probation and finally a prison sentence. A number of them become involved in organised crime and 'succeed' in being sentenced to imprisonment during the winter months, to return to the streets when summer comes round again. Prisons and psychiatric hospitals are being increasingly used as places of refuge by homeless youths.

There is a further category. Young people who have been taken care of in children's homes until the time for their discharge are found employment and they start off in a suitable flat. All goes well for some time but, being alone and lonely as well as rootless, they begin to drift. Formerly many of these got satisfactory live-in jobs in hospitals or private houses. With increasing unemployment such jobs are no longer available. This is another group of homeless young sorely in need of adequate after-care service.

Priority should be given to a short-stay assessment unit in Cork. Other services needed are a short-stay hostel for homeless boys, a residential unit for teenage girls, a residential treatment centre for young addicts, suitable accommodation for travellers, hostel accommodation for extremely problematic and homeless boys, residential centre for teenage boys who cannot cope with the open setting of a training centre and who need a whole range of back-up services, psychiatric services for under-eighteens.


**CO-ORDINATING BODY**
The greatest challenge facing the providers of care now is in the area of preventative measures, and this is an area where the voluntary organisations give of their best. But there is a pressing need to establish a national forum which would enable the voluntary bodies who work in the field to liaise with the Department of Health in the preventative, custodial and after-care services. Our ideal as a caring society should be to see that no one is left in dire need in our midst, but without co-ordination at national level this proposal cannot even get off the ground. It is essential that the state should assume responsibility for the homeless in all areas, and that it does not oblige the already

over-worked, under-staffed and under-financed voluntary organisations to shoulder responsibility in these vital areas of social concern. The present situation, whereby the health boards have the main responsibility but yet no real voice in policy decisions, especially in the area of housing provisions, is entirely unsatisfactory as a means to providing a lasting solution to the problem of homelessness.

by Marie Murphy SGS

# Youth Work Responses to Young People Out-of-Home

## The Role of Youth Work and Other Services

**THE EXTENT OF THE PROBLEM**

Figures from Focus-Point, a Dublin-based organisation dealing with the homeless, for the period September 1985 to September 1986 indicate that their outreach team, which consists of two full-time workers with support from voluntary part-time people, were in contact with 211 people who were homeless or unattached. Of this group 144 were under twenty-two years of age and of these some thirty-three were under sixteen. The majority of these people were living in temporary or insecure situations: they were sleeping rough, dossing or living in hostels. Nearly half of them were identified as having serious personal difficulties such as alcohol abuse, drug abuse or psychiatric illness. Nearly all were unemployed.

The National Campaign for the Homeless carried out a survey of Ireland's young homeless in 1984. That survey identified 800 young homeless people nationally. Of these 531 were aged under twenty years and 410 were aged between twenty and thirty. Most had become homeless because of family break-up. Homelessness was often associated with substance abuse.

These are only the figures for homeless people who could be identified through contact with agencies. It is reasonable to assume that the problem is significantly worse than the figures portray.

I have consulted also with some community-based youth workers and with people running community training workshops. I was keen to establish the extent to which they came across or had heard of young people in their community who had been living out of their homes at some time. It was not perceived to be a common occurrence, but my contacts were aware that the issue exists and that it is something that is mainly hidden. Generally, their experience was that young people who left home usually did so temporarily, as a result of a crisis, and usually managed to stay with a friend or series of friends or with a close relative. Usually the young person was able to find some form of temporary accommodation, though in many cases this was after they had spent a few nights sleeping rough.

A number of important issues arise from this. Firstly, homelessness — temporary or long-term — often arises from an inability on the part of the young person to cope with their family situation. Secondly, the supports which are available to the young person are initially sought within their own community. And thirdly, the role of the personal friendship network and close relatives living nearby are of major significance. I believe that a properly developed community-based youth service could be a major resource for young people who have difficulty living at home.

## EDUCATION AGAINST HOMELESSNESS
I do not see homelessness as an issue in itself. It is in the majority of cases a symptom of the difficulties affecting a young person. Any effort to deal with homelessness must look at the real personal needs of the individual and the issues that affect their lives. In a minority of cases simply finding a flat or some alternative accommodation will be all that is required, but any attempt really to deal with the issues of homelessness must look at the total needs of the person, with their consent, of course.

It is generally expected of all young people that they will eventually leave the family home. Young people are expected to grow to become autonomous, independent individuals capable of finding their own place within the community. Most young people achieve autonomy with relative ease and with appropriate support from family and others, but in times of growing unemployment and significant rapid social change, the chances of many young people making this transition in a satisfactory fashion are reduced. Young people who come from economically, emotionally or socially disadvantaged situations have the greatest difficulty in making this transition.

Generally speaking, there is relatively little education for young people in the process of leaving home. Education on this theme should be included in life skills programmes in all second-level schools. (Elements of this type of programme are occasionally included in the curriculum of transition year students.) Even if such a programme were developed within schools it would not cater for the ongoing educational needs of the young person who leaves school early. It is in meeting the needs of this type of young person that I see the youth service making a significant contribution.

## COMMUNITY PROGRAMMES
Within the catchment area of the Dublin Youth Service Board (Comhairle le Leas Óige) with which I am employed, there are ten community-based programmes currently in operation. Each of these programmes employs full-time youth workers, eighteen in all. These programmes are supported and monitored by An Chomhairle le Leas Óige, and where they are located within

99

a particular community, the community is closely involved with the development and management of the programme. I believe that these youth development programmes can play a crucial role in providing support and education to young people who come into contact with them. In fact, the youth development programmes are in the unique position of being able to reach out and make contact with 'unattached' young people. The informal role of unattached youth workers, along with very detailed local knowledge and community support, provides the youth worker with an ideal opportunity to be a significant resource to young people who are at risk of becoming homeless. The programmes which are currently being developed and run within communities provide a unique potential for an appropriate response to the needs of these young people. In addition, these youth workers can provide useful training resources for local people which can facilitate a real community response.

There have been some interesting new developments in finding relevant approaches to the identification of potentially homeless young people in the Manchester area of England. In essence they developed preventative educational programmes, which were carried out in youth clubs and in community youth projects and drop-in centres which were involved with unattached young people. It is, I think, reasonable to assume that there is a great deal of similarity between the needs of young people in large urban and suburban housing estates in England and Ireland, and that we can learn from their experience. Essentially, they developed education programmes on the theme of learning about the process of leaving home. The programme was developed around full-time youth workers in youth centres and part-time and voluntary youth workers and leaders, the central idea being to explore the whole process of leaving home. I will outline the aims and objectives of the programme, because I believe much of it will be applicable in many of the three hundred youth groups which are currently registered with Comhairle le Leas Óige. The aims and objectives of the programme are to:

- help towards the recognition of the educational role that youth workers can play in preparing young people for leaving home

- increase understanding of the way in which young people perceive the issue of homelessness or leaving home and to discover where they may need information and skills in order to survive and succeed

- help young people to clarify their own ideas about leaving home and to test out the reality of the situation

- help young people and those involved in youth work to identify ways in which they can collect practical information and advice to help someone leaving home

100

- explore the relationship between youth work and homelessness and to examine whether this is an issue with which youth workers and voluntary youth leaders should concern themselves

I believe that An Chomhairle le Leas Óige is very well placed to develop and implement such a programme in the Dublin city area.

## A ROLE FOR YOUTH WORKERS

One of the most significant roles that youth workers can play is that of co-ordinating the efforts of the agencies which operate in the communities, particularly where these agencies are operating in the interests of young people who are disadvantaged. I am referring mainly to community schemes operating in conjunction with AnCO, YEA, Teamwork schemes, etc, which, although temporary, provide a potential developmental vehicle for the young person. Skilled and sensitive use of these opportunities is currently happening in many communities and, if applied in an appropriate way, they could prove to be very beneficial to those most in need.

Agencies such as the Probation and Welfare Service, the juvenile liaison scheme of the Garda Síochána, special residential schools, hostels for young homeless, and many other agencies have a potentially invaluable resource at their disposal, through contact with full-time youth workers operating in communities, as these workers are often the only acceptable link with societal institutions that are available to the young person who is potentially at risk or homeless. The local youth worker can play a really significant co-ordinating role in relation to those agencies and can hopefully reduce the confusion experienced by the young person through contact with numerous professionals from different agencies. Proper co-ordination of efforts can, I believe, result in a more appropriate response to the needs of the young person and facilitate a better use of resources. Familiarity with all of the agencies which are likely to be resourceful to the potentially homeless young persons is an essential requirement of community youth workers.

## ENCOURAGING DEVELOPMENTS

There have been some encouraging developments recently in the area of responding to the needs of young homeless people in Dublin. Developments such as the funding of Focus-Point by the Dublin Youth Service Board to enable them to employ two full-time outreach workers indicate that there is an important role to be played by the Youth Service in meeting the needs of young people who are living out-of-home. The results of the work of the outreach team in conjunction with the other services of Focus-Point are obvious to anyone who is familiar with their operation.

The recent appointment by the Eastern Health Board of five full-time workers whose role, I understand, is in the area of supporting young homeless people is to be welcomed. These appointments represent a potentially significant advance.

CO-ORDINATION AND INTEGRATION
I believe this potential can only be maximised if the workers' roles are integrated with existing agencies operating in this field in addition to people operating at community level. These recent developments seem to be sporadic, and the many agencies involved, both voluntary and statutory, are not in sufficiently close contact to ensure the co-ordinated development of services. I believe that a properly co-ordinated policy which takes account of the aims and objectives of agencies such as AnCO, City of Dublin VEC, Comhairle le Leas Óige, Youth Employment Agency, Department of Labour Teamwork schemes, Department of Justice Probation and Welfare Service, Eastern Health Board, at community level, could make a really significant contribution towards planning proper educational interventions and towards optimising the complementary roles that are currently being played by these organisations.

Many of these agencies are operating in the educational domain, each trying to meet specific needs often with the same participants. A properly co-ordinated and integrated education policy geared towards providing learning opportunities in vocational preparation and life skills, taking account of the needs of people for everyday living, is likely to create a population that is better equipped to deal with the demands of living today and might address issues relating to the issues of homelessness.

If such an integrated policy doesn't evolve we will continue to have an *ad hoc* development of services to young people at community level, particularly in relation to young people with the greatest needs. Resources are woefully scarce in terms of personnel, finance, services and buildings to cater for potentially and actually homeless people. It is essential that, where resources exist, they are used to maximum effect.

ACCOMMODATION FOR OUT-OF-HOME YOUTH
One practical step which would provide an immediate, though by no means total, solution to the needs of homeless persons would be to give effect to the Housing (Miscellaneous Provisions) Bill 1985 which places statutory responsibility on local housing authorities to make an annual assessment of housing needs of such groups as the homeless and other vulnerable categories in need, as well as the requirement to make provision.

The national youth policy, *In Partnership with Youth* (1985), stated that it is the responsibility of the health boards to provide for long-term and short-stay accommodation for homeless young people and that each local authority and health board would nominate an official from within their approved staff complement to liaise with each other and with the voluntary bodies in their areas involved with the homeless to effect a co-ordinated response to the needs in this area. In addition, the policy states that small-scale residential units with adequate care provisions rather than large-scale institutional care is desirable. It also states that face-to-face youth workers and drop-in centres will be employed in some areas as back-up services to homeless young people as part of the national youth service. Clearly, some progress has been made in relation to the above; however, there is much yet to be implemented.

The most basic physical and safety needs of homeless young people can be met through the provision of suitable hostel or residential accommodation. The recent opening of the short-term boys' hostel at Percy Place, Dublin, is a welcome resource, but the hostel cannot meet the needs of young people who may require longer-term accommodation along with suitable levels of support geared to the particular needs of the individual young person.

Emergency accommodation is essential but for many it isn't enough. An additional type of provision is needed, which is obliged to cater for young persons irrespective of their behaviour patterns and which can offer the relevant type of support. It seems that the most appropriate agency for this type of provision within the Dublin region is the Eastern Health Board.

To increase the likelihood of being a real and appropriate resource to the young person out-of-home who is being accommodated in a hostel it is essential that

- the overall needs of the young person are assessed, not just their accommodation requirements
- a plan of action is developed which is appropriate to these needs
- the plan is implemented
- when the young person returns to his or her community a suitable and appropriate level of support of an ongoing nature is implemented and the ongoing process is monitored

It is preferable that hostels should be located as close to the young person's local environment as possible to minimise the trauma. Hence the need for a small number of suitable types of accommodation in different areas of the city.

103

I am not suggesting that each young person who is out-of-home is in need of constant support indefinitely. Many will return to families with relative ease and with simple appropriate support, but the needs of people out-of-home will vary and so will the level of support.

**A RESPONSE TO THE NEEDS OF THE POTENTIALLY LONG-TERM HOMELESS**
The final area which I would like to address is that of developing a response to the young people who drift into the city centre and who involve themselves in a way of life that is likely to increase their chances of becoming homeless in the long term. The outreach team from Focus-Point has managed to make contact with many of these young people, but this contact cannot reach its full potential unless the outreach workers have appropriate resources to meet the real needs of these homeless young people. The whole purpose of making contact is to develop a working relationship between the outreach worker and the young person, which will operate to the advantage of the young person.

It seems to me that there is a need for a drop-in centre in the city centre which can provide a comfortable and non-threatening resource to the young person and which will operate on the basis of providing opportunities with 'no strings attached'. I am of the opinion that such a centre, staffed by properly trained workers and properly resourced, could be an invaluable response to some of their needs. Such a centre should be able to offer information and learning experiences which are appropriate to the needs of the young person. It should offer opportunities for involvement and should respect their right to self-determination. Consideration should be given by both voluntary and statutory agencies to the idea of providing this type of centre and suitable programmes to operate within it should be drawn up.

**CONCLUSION**
What is needed now is a community-based structure to operate as an educational and preventative measure, proper co-ordination of agencies concerned with young people, legislation responding to the issues of homelessness and adequate resources.

by Derry O'Connor

# Homeless Young People and Drug Use

Is drug use a primary problem which leads to parental rejection or runaway behaviour, or is it merely another symptom of more general psycho-social problems? Is it necessary to focus explicitly on the drug problems of homeless young people and should the helping services be provided by specialists in drug problems?

Drug use is only one factor in homelessness amongst the young: the drug-taking habits of the young are unlikely to be the main reason for their homelessness, just as homelessness itself is not caused by a literal shortage of bricks and mortar, though we all agree that an immediate and primary need among the homeless is for some form of physical shelter. Rather than asking what causes homelessness in young people, we would do better to try to find out their needs and to see what the strengths and weaknesses of their families, schools and communities have in terms of meeting these needs.

## UNDERSTANDING DRUG USE

The drugs we are concerned with here vary considerably in terms of their legality, the health hazards they create and their ability to bring about behavioural change; what they have in common is that they all bring about mood change and have the capacity to create physical and/or psychological addiction, a state in which drug use is compulsive rather than by choice. The use of mood-altering drugs is common in all cultures and has been since time immemorial. All such drug use cannot be categorised as culturally deviant or objectively problematic.

Drug use is relatively common among young people, and a number of surveys of post-primary school pupils in Ireland have indicated that drug use is a common (although still a minority) practice. The most recent of these surveys[1] shows the following facts among post-primary pupils in the Dublin area:

- Two-thirds had smoked cigarettes at some time in their lives, more than one-third had smoked in the month prior to the survey and almost one-quarter described themselves as regular smokers.

- Two-thirds had taken a whole alcoholic drink at some time in their lives, nearly half had done so in the month prior to survey and more than one-third were regular drinkers.

- The use of other drugs was less common, with volatile substances (such as glues and aerosols) and marijuana being most popular. About 13 per cent of the sample had tried each of these substances and about 8 per cent had used these or another illicit substance in the previous month.

Not all drug use is problematic. We can categorise drug use in the following way. *Experimental* drug use refers to occasional, poorly planned use which is aimed at testing out a substance or an experience. This is a typical feature of all adolescent behaviour. *Recreational* drug use is a more regular occurrence and is more carefully planned. *Addictive* drug use is compulsive and is carried out in a chaotic manner, often to the detriment of the user's most fundamental human needs.

Addictive drug use is the most risky form of drug use, but there is a common-sense recognition that all three categories are potentially hazardous. It is sometimes said that an individual young person who experiments with solvents is at greater risk than an individual who uses solvents recreationally with a gang of peers; the gang is more likely to have built up some lore or culture on the risks involved, while the isolated youngster may inadvertently kill himself or herself through sheer ignorance.

Drug use among teenagers is, of course, frowned upon by adult society and there are some specific legal sanctions, such as the law prohibiting the sale of tobacco and alcohol to minors in addition to the Misuse of Drugs Acts which apply to all age groups. On the face of it, it would seem likely that teenagers who violate these norms concerning drug use are errant or disaffected in other ways and not just in this isolated area. Grube and Morgan[1] have reported that students with a low level of drug use were more committed to and involved with their family, school and church. Another recent study from the south of England[2] has found a significant association between drug use among teenagers and three social factors — having an unemployed father, having an absent parent and belonging to a larger family — which are also associated with general delinquency in this age group. This study also indicated that drug use, including under-age drinking and smoking, is significantly associated with vandalism, truancy and fighting.

### CHILDREN OUT-OF-HOME AND DRUGS
Adolescence and young adulthood is a difficult transitional period, not merely for the young person who is attempting to individuate, but also for his or her family. Other problems in the family and social environment, such as poverty, mental illness, alcohol abuse, or poor housing, add to the difficulties of this period. When young people become 'vagrant', 'homeless', 'unattached' or whatever word we choose to use, it is obvious that they themselves do not have the personal maturity or strength to resolve their problems. More importantly, these young people have not been adequately supported by the informal (family, extended family, neighbourhood and wider community) and formal (educational, social and medical services) networks that surround them. They have not developed to the point where they can take charge of their own lives, although they appear to have lost faith in parental and all other conventional authority.

106

Young people of this kind are obviously vulnerable in all kinds of ways. Their long-term prospects seem poor, given that they have no chance to develop normally, in social and emotional terms, and no chance to educate or train themselves so that they can compete for jobs with their peers. They seem destined for life-long disturbance, with an excessive amount of contact with prisons, mental hospitals and the social services. This is a pattern which, unless effective helping services are provided, can be seen to emerge while they are still in their teens.

It seems that drug use among homeless young people is only one of several problems causing and/or caused by homelessness. The Dún Laoghaire Drug Awareness Group, a voluntary organisation, has in the past year done some work with a group of streetchildren. They had little or no bonding to adult authority figures, they had literacy problems, were involved in constant petty crime, indiscriminate use of drugs (including alcohol) and premature sexual activity. Their drug use consisted primarily of drinking and use of volatile substances — glue, lighter fuel, petrol and other substances of this kind — although some had dabbled with harder drugs. In addition to the risks of overdosing or accidental injury or death while intoxicated, young drug users now face the new hazard of exposure to the AIDS virus.

### SERVICES FOR HOMELESS YOUNG DRUG USERS
It appears that homeless young people constitute both a high drug user and a high risk group. In other words, this group is more likely to suffer casualties because it is so vulnerable in many ways, and also because drug use in this group is unusually high.

The most immediate need for homeless young people is for shelter, somewhere they can sleep, eat, wash and talk to stable, caring adults. The dilemmas facing helpers presented with homeless young people who are intoxicated are comparable to those faced by workers in adult shelters, such as Simon. There is a reluctance to refuse help to people who are intoxicated, yet there is a depressing sense that little can be done while clients persist in using drugs, and a fear that non-using clients will be upset or led into drug use if constantly exposed to users. There is no single, simple answer to this dilemma: much depends on the physical facilities and staffing resources available to agencies. Sometimes it is possible to offer basic shelter to young users, at other times it appears necessary to exclude them. Medical assessment, detoxification and treatment of physical damage may be necessary, although conventional drug treatment services are primarily geared towards the adult population.

Homeless young people, whether they use drugs or not, should not be labelled as young vagrants, that is as young people who have permanently abandoned their commitment to and involvement with family, friends, local community and local helping services. Some social service administrators have a tendency to do this, and to see homeless young people as being in need of nothing more than shelter — while they are waiting to become adult vagrants and eligible for the services for vagrant adults. Homeless young people need much more than shelter; in particular, they need to be helped to re-establish connections with family and extended family, and, where appropriate, helped to move back home. The fact that young people are designated as 'homeless' or 'drug addicts', or indeed as both, should not justify their abandonment by the primary health and social service team.

There has in the past been an excessive mystique surrounding drug problems and a belief in the need for and effectiveness of specialised treatment services. This point of view is being increasingly challenged, and local generic services are coming to be seen as having major advantages over centralised, specialist services. While it is undoubtedly true that some homeless teenage drug users would benefit from specialised rehabilitation, such as that provided by therapeutic communities, it is equally clear that the majority of such young-sters are not prepared to enter treatment services which are intensive and demanding of a high degree of motivation. Not all young users are addicts and it is inappropriate to try to fit them into treatment programmes designed for addicts.

Young drug users who live rough need a range of services, provided flexibly and with a high degree of co-ordination and co-operation among the carers. Streetwork which involves making contact with such young people and making them aware of the helping agencies, is important. The Hope service was moving in this direction prior to its closure and the Ana Liffey project currently does some streetwork. If such services are uncoordinated, there is an obvious risk of resources being wasted and needs being unmet. It would seem sensible that the health boards, specifically the community care social work teams, should be given the task of co-ordinating these services. Equally, it seems necessary that individual clients should still remain the primary res-ponsibility of the social worker for the area from which they originate. The families of origin of these youngsters are usually problematic (frequently with parental alcoholism as an important contributory factor), and there is a temptation to write them off as being beyond changing or being helped.

CONCLUSIONS
Drug use among young people, as among adults, is common and has the potential for creating many problems and exacerbating existing problems. In the case of young people who are drifting away from parents, family and the

usual social supports, drug use can be a significant feature of the total picture. Help should be offered with a view to maintaining some connection with family of origin, extended family and local community, while at the same time recognising the primary need for shelter. Services for this particular group should be co-ordinated by local health board social workers, although they may involve many voluntary agencies. While workers should be aware of the risk posed by drug use and should attempt to minimise these risks, they should not see referral to specialist drug rehabilitation services as the most logical or desirable procedure.

by Shane Butler

1. Joel Grube and Mark Morgan (1986), *Smoking, Drinking and Other Drug Use Among Dublin Post-Primary School Pupils*, Dublin: Economic and Social Research Institute.
2. Colin Pritchard, Mary Fielding, N. Choudry, Malcolm Cox and Ian Diamond (1986), Incidence of drug and solvent abuse in 'normal' fourth and fifth year comprehensive school children — some socio-behavioural characteristics, *British Journal of Social Work* 16, 341-51.

# Focus-Point's Outreach Service

Focus-Point is a self-help resource centre, providing an information and advice centre, settlement service, coffee-shop/restaurant, twenty-four-hour emergency telephone line, creative activity centre for women and children, research, communication, a house of hospitality and an outreach or streetwork service. This outreach service is aimed to provide a special service for disaffiliated and unattached young people.

Special services to youth is defined in the national youth policy committee's report (1985) as including drop-in and advice and information centres, neighbourhood projects, youth encounter and detached youth work. Detached youth work is another way of describing outreach work or streetwork. Outreach work is not highly developed in this country, though centre-based youth work has developed considerably, with drop-in, information and activity centres. Indeed, outreach work is often seen as an early stage in the setting up of centre-based activities, and is discontinued once the centre has been established. We in the Focus-Point outreach service, however, see our outreach work as a particular and distinct form of youth work, based not in centres but on the streets.

The Focus-Point outreach service made a decision to give priority to under-twenty-fives, as the Simon community tends to concentrate on the older age-group. Our work is aimed at 'unattached' youth — young people unattached both physically and emotionally from their families, from concerned adults and youth workers, and even from other young people, and who are living out-of-home and with no alternative secure accommodation.

Our outreach service has to fit into the environment of a commercial city centre area where neither worker nor young person has a history, friendship, peer-group or family or local connections. We are not centre-based but meet young people on the streets. We are involved with a particularly vulnerable section of the youth population — those who are out-of-home — a mobile and changing group.

### OBJECTIVES
The objectives of the outreach team are as follows:

- to make and maintain contact with young people who are out-of-home and unattached in the city centre
- to provide the young people with the resources they lack as a result of being out-of-home
- to build a profile of young people's experience out-of-home and on the streets
- to contribute to the development of policy and services to meet their needs

How we meet these objectives is described below.

### MAKING CONTACT
We make contact with the young out-of-home in structured situations such as hostels, day centres, dinner houses, drop-in centres, and in unstructured situations such as pool halls, arcades, fast food restaurants, street corners, parks, and it is in such unstructured environments that most of our contact is made and maintained.

We begin by spending time in these places, getting to know the staff, customers, letting people know what we do and gradually becoming accepted as a part of life in that scene. We then identify those young people who are out-of-home from those merely passing through. It is only over a long time that we gain any understanding of what it is like for them to be out-of-home, and we need the flexibility to be able to spend time with those who are drifting in the city centre. On making contact we offer friendly and non-

110

threatening company, where respect, interest, trust and sharing are key factors. We address the fear young people surviving on the streets have by being clear about our purpose, by making ourselves available to them at times and in places that fit the momentum of their lives, rather than imposing ourselves on them. We use peer groups and other informal networks as a means of introduction rather than intruding upon them.

## PROVIDING RESOURCES
Sometimes we find we are the only responsible adults available to such young people. We work at overcoming their sense of isolation by providing a connection with the support networks they lack because they are out-of-home, and we advocate on behalf of young people, referring them to other agencies when necessary.

Acceptance, support and counselling over a long period of time at a pace dictated by their experience of life can help to counter the chaotic feelings of anger, fear, confusion, loneliness and hopelessness experienced by young people out-of-home. The final stage is gradually disengaging from those we have worked with. This is difficult, as relationships are often long-lasting and significant to the young people.

## POLICY ISSUES
We have communicated with different statutory and voluntary agencies about individual people, and have enabled them to receive the assistance and service they require and are entitled to. We have identified a number of gaps in current service provision. The particular issues that we have raised are:

- the need for an alternative short-term and emergency hostel after the closure of Hope hostel (This need has been partly met with the opening of Percy Place.)

- the fact that homeless young people both over and under eighteen exist and in much greater numbers than statutory agencies recognise

- the involvement of young people, male and female and under and over sixteen, in prostitution and the inability or unwillingness of various statutory agencies to intervene

- the involvement of young homeless people, both from the Travelling and from the settled community, in regular solvent abuse and the inability of existing addiction agencies to meet their needs

111

**BUILDING UP A PROFILE**

The flexibility of the outreach project enables us to spend time with young people on their own ground and record accurately and sensitively what they have to say. The process of finding out what it is like to be out-of-home, the difficulties, sense of isolation, powerlessness and exclusion experienced by the young people, cannot be achieved in a month or two. The seven different groupings of young people who are out-of-home, unattached and who identify with a street subculture that we describe here are the result of work over a period of a year in which we gained a picture of life for young people on the streets by documentation and regular evaluation of our work.

GROUP 1 YOUNG WOMEN OUT-OF-HOME

This group consisted of four friends between sixteen and seventeen years of age who were out-of-home for six months when first met by the outreach team. They spent most of their time in the O'Connell Street and Henry Street area, meeting boyfriends, shop-lifting, playing pool, doing 'runners' for drug dealers. They slept in the homes and flats of different friends, in cars or squats in the north inner city.

Contact was first made with this group by following up a phone call to the emergency phone-in service, and during the following months a strong supportive relationship was built up with two of the girls. When crises occurred the outreach team was contacted.

On contact, three of these young women had serious drug addiction problems, all four had used the existing hostel services and family ties were at very best tenuous. We were a source of information, advice and support in very difficult circumstances over a long period.

The group no longer exists: two are still using drugs and have been in prison for long periods, one is in psychiatric care and the fourth is involved in prostitution. The longer these young women continue to abuse drugs, remain involved in prostitution, move from place to place, serve longer prison sentences, the further removed they become from social service agencies and the more difficult it is for them to break out of the cycle of homelessness.

GROUP 2 YOUNG WOMEN OUT-OF-HOME

This group of eight young women ranging in age from fourteen to twenty-five were part of a bigger group comprising about twenty people under twenty-two, who were sleeping rough in the city centre and with whom we had contact from October 1985 to April 1986. They had been sleeping rough and dossing for about six to eight months on our contact with them. A core group of four women, with another four on the periphery, spent

112

most of their time in the Grafton Street and Middle Abbey Street area, particularly in coffee shops. They slept in squats and flats and on the street
with members of the larger group. The group offered an opportunity to
experiment with drugs, relationships and living on the streets.

Contact with this group was initiated through relationships built primarily
with men in the larger group. The majority of the women were very sub-
servient to the demands of the men in the group.

In contrast to the first group of young women, this group managed, with
substantial intervention from the outreach team, to move out of the cycle
of long-term homelessness. We helped them to find accommodation of their
own and supported them in this and in their relationships. All but two of
them have settled in satisfactory accommodation with continued support
from the outreach team.

GROUP 3 BOYS ON THEIR OWN
This group consists of eleven boys under eighteen who spend most of their
time on their own. While most of the boys know each other, they do not
hang around together like other groups, nor do they mix with other groups
on the streets. This makes it difficult for the team to meet their friends and
initial contact is often made on a person-to-person basis rather than meeting
a group.

Six of the boys were out-of-home approximately four months when first
encountered by the outreach team and over the past four months, six other
boys have become known to us. They spend a lot of time in amusement
arcades, pool halls in the Westmoreland Street, O'Connell Street, Eden Quay
area. At night they sleep in cars, doorways and with acquaintances.

A high percentage of this young group become involved in prostitution soon
after they become homeless. Intervention with this group is very difficult
because of their youth, their vulnerability and their involvement in prostitution. We have helped them by establishing:

- long-term supportive relationships with individuals while they stay out-
  of-home
- liaison with health board social workers to find suitable care
- regular contact and presence on the streets

The majority of the original group have now left the streets as a direct result of the contact with the outreach team. Three have been placed in the care of the health board and two have returned home.

GROUP 4 PUNKS
The punk group is perhaps the most obvious of the youth groupings in the city centre. They comprise a core group of six young men with another six young men and two young women joining the group at weekends or on special occasions. The punk subculture offers valid expression to an alternative and anti-social lifestyle that revolves around a code of dress and music interests geared to shock 'straight' members of society. Members of the punk group who remain in the city centre after others have moved on represent the more marginalised section of this subculture. Family problems, alcoholism, addiction and homelessness with a lack of intervention from relevant agencies has resulted in long-term problems for many young people in this group.

Contact with the group was initiated through intensive work with one member of the group within a structured situation. This led to meetings with other members over a period of four months. Contact with members of this group was sometimes intermittent and sometimes intensive because of seasonal changes. At present most of the young members have left Dublin for London and may return in the summer. Our contact continues with remaining members of the group.

GROUP 5 DRIFTERS
While this group of twenty young men and women is informal and undefined, it was long-lasting and played an important part in the lives of its members. It fulfilled four great needs — acceptance, accommodation, information and structure to their lives. Women within the group assumed and were placed in traditional roles for much of the time: any activities particular to the women themselves were segregated. The group formed through members sharing a number of squats or 'open' flats and was strengthened by their gathering daily in a few coffee shops in the city centre. Open flats and squats fulfilled the immediate need for accommodation of its members, but also perpetuated their homelessness. It was very difficult for members to maintain flats because the rest of the group always arrived and this led inevitably to eviction.

Our intervention had only a slight effect until four members of the group began to make use of our service and asked us to help them to get accommodation. Suddenly the image of the streetboys lost approval. A home of one's own became fashionable. Many members found accommodation, while those who could not make a change drifted into other groups. Since then some of these homes have broken down again, the task of running a

114

flat has been too much for some who have few social and living skills. The rest have become more stable and settled in their new accommodation.

## GROUP 6 OLDER MEN'S DRINKING GROUP
This group comprises the forty younger men of a larger group of men who are out-of-home and use the night shelters, dinner halls and other traditional provisions for the homeless. While the framework of this group has existed for many years, members participate in the group for two to nine months. Subgroups are constantly forming and dissolving within the larger group. Relationships within the group tend to be shallow and transient. The common experience of using services for the homeless, such as night shelters and dinner centres, brought the group together. Daily life follows an institutionalised routine of waiting and moving from one accommodation to the next, from one dinner centre to the next. Low esteem and hopelessness characterise the feelings of many of the group. The group follows a circular pattern with members coming to use the night shelters and moving between them at regular intervals. We have referred many members of this group to the advice/information section of Focus-Point which has assisted them with their accommodation and social welfare problems.

## GROUP 7 YOUNG TRAVELLERS
Our contact with these nineteen Travellers out-of-home began on meeting them as part of a larger group of young people from the settled population who were sleeping rough. Over the past year our contact has intensified. The number of young Travellers we meet has increased, as has the frequency of our contact with them. The average age of this group is fourteen and a large number are solvent abusers. Because the conditions under which the Travellers are forced to live renders them a marginalised and greatly disadvantaged group, children from this community who leave home have even fewer options. The majority of those we have met over the past year spent a lot of time, day and night in the city centre. A number return home at night but approximately eleven have been sleeping rough over the past six months.

Intervention began with two young Travellers who spent a lot of time with a group from the settled population, sleeping out. Here our role was in the main friendship, advice and liaison with relevant agencies to meet their needs. The options open to this group are even more limited because of the disadvantaged position Travellers have in our society.

## CONCLUSION
The young people we have worked with were unable or unwilling to use the services of Focus-Point or other agencies on their own initiative, and often we were the only responsible adults in contact with them. Outreach work is

thus not only innovative but an important and valid aspect of youth work, with its own skills, processes and methods. Outreach work can only operate in an agency setting that provides it with support and can allow it the flexibility to develop and change.

All the young people we are in contact with have certain basic needs that current services are unable to address adequately. There are variations in the services required, according to the age and dependency of the young person. Recommendations to meet these needs are outlined at the end of this book together with recommendations made by other contributors (pp. 148).

by Majella Mulkeen and Shane Sheridan

We would like to thank the staff of Focus-Point especially Justin O'Brien for their help in preparing this paper. We would also like to pay particular tribute to the young homeless people from whom we have learned most of what is written here.

# Young Travellers on the Streets of Dublin

## International Year of Shelter for the Homeless and Travellers

I have serious reservations about the good that this International Year of Shelter for the Homeless can do for the Travelling people in the Dublin area. The International Year of the Child (1979) promised something in the nature of a children's crusade, but it ended up as a street-cleaning exercise, with housing welfare officers actually suggesting that Travelling streetchildren should be locked up in secure units. The attitude of officials does not seem any more helpful now: when Sr Brenda O'Neill asked what Dublin Corporation proposed to do for the Travelling people in this international year, the reply from the city fathers was that it was all very well to nominate international years, but that 'these people' didn't have to deal with Travellers on a day-to-day basis.

There is a danger that this international year will be just as disastrous, and that even this seminar will be no more than a talking shop, producing what I call the three academic Rs — reports, resolutions and recommendations — but no action. In a way this sort of exercise allows us caring professionals to feel involved and caring, but at the same time to remain remote from the realities, much as other people get a comfortable feeling from giving a few coppers to Travelling children begging on a cold day. But gestures like this will not change the situation.

According to an ESRI report of 1986, the Dublin area is the bleakest with regard to Travellers, although it is also the area where the greatest number of social workers is employed working directly with Travellers. In the Dublin area we have a good number of staff employed by the Eastern Health Board, Dublin County Council, Dublin Corporation and the voluntary Dublin Committee for Travelling People, but there seems to be little action to show for the number of workers and the number of reviews, research projects and resolutions generated in the area.

### THE SITUATION OF TRAVELLERS
There are more Travellers on the roadside now than at any time since settlement began in the 1960s. Few local authorities have provided for the Travellers

in their areas, and no local authority has provided for the projected growth in family numbers.

LIVING CONDITIONS
In the Dublin Eastern Health Board area 50 per cent of Travellers have no piped water and 75 per cent have no hot tap water; 62 per cent have no access to toilet facilities of any kind. Roadside Travellers have no access to electricity and 36 per cent of Travellers live in over-crowded conditions in families of ten or more people.

MORTALITY
The following table compares the child mortality rates in the Travelling and settled population:

| Travellers | Settled population |
|---|---|
| 14.2% under 1 year | 2.3% under 1 year |
| 25.0% under 5 years | 2.8% under 5 years |
| 31.8% under 10 years | 3.1% under 10 years |
| 35.9% under 15 years | 3.4% under 15 years |

Only 5.5 per cent of Travellers and 4.6 per cent of roadside Travellers are over fifty years of age, as compared with about 23.5% of the population as a whole, and of the 13,201 Travellers whose age was known in 1981, only 210, or 1.6 per cent were over sixty-five. The reason for this high mortality rate among young Travellers is the failure of the local authorities to provide enough standard, healthy housing and prejudice is an important reason behind this failure.

EDUCATION
As well as being denied the basic right to healthy living conditions in an atmosphere that respects their way of life, free of discrimination from the settled community and from officialdom, Travellers also have poor access to education. About 90 per cent of Travellers are illiterate and only one-third of Travelling children of school-going age are at school. The single greatest reason for non-attendance at school is lack of accommodation.

**CONCLUSION**
I find it hard to see how we can read the UN Declaration of the Rights of the Child and not squirm at the inadequate child-care, youth and social service, educational outlets and future life chances for the majority of working-class and Travelling children in this country. How can we reflect on the aspirations of the constitution and at the same time accept as a matter

of fact the statistics I have quoted here with regard to Travellers? Have social and community workers lost their edge and their sense of outrage? If there is any chance of anything good coming out of this seminar, it is that we listen to the Travellers themselves rather than to the 'brokers' and it is to this end that I now introduce the next section, the experience of a young Travelling woman told in her own words.

by Mervyn Ennis

# Experiences of a Traveller

I myself started begging shortly after my family moved near the centre of the city. Being on the streets looking for pity from other people who worked hard for a living was not my idea of living, but at that time there wasn't much for me or the other young Travellers to do except sit on the street day after day. After a while I kind of got sick of the whole idea of it and tried to ask myself why I was doing it and what was the meaning of it. I soon came up with a few answers. I didn't always think about begging because I had my parents and a family so I wasn't all that bad. For one thing I wasn't alone because I had my friends and someone to turn to. But still I was on the street begging at that time.

One day early in December one of my friends told me about an all-Travellers course coming up. She also told me there was no harm in trying to put in for it, that it was better than sitting on the streets. She asked me to give it a thought so I did and I told myself there was nothing to lose.

I can't tell you how really excited I felt and so were the other young Travellers. The aim of the course was to get young Travellers to develop their skills as leaders. The course started in January and finished the following July. Throughout the course I really felt great because I was learning and I also felt I had something to look forward to every morning. I called it a job.

Being on the course I hadn't to beg on the streets, because I was a member of a project and that's where I thought I should be. But coming to the end I kind of got nerves again, for there were no promises that we would get anything at the end of it. The course organisers John and Ronnie just couldn't guarantee us anything but just said we might as well keep our hopes up.

At the time the last thing I wanted to think of was going back to the streets

119

begging. The course finished with tears and sadness and we hoped we would get the funding from the Department of Labour so that we could set something up for us Travellers who had nothing else better to be doing with our time. Shortly after we finished there wasn't much for me to do but go back to the street begging.

In September it all began for me — trouble which I thought would never be solved. We had home problems and very serious ones. In spite of the problems I still hoped I would get another job on Teamwork which John and Ronnie had mentioned before we finished the course. That month I was expecting John or Ronnie because they said if they got the funding for Teamwork they would let us know some time in September. Any day that month I was expecting them.

It happened just the way I thought about inside me. It was coming to the end of the month, the weather was really beautiful. It was a sunny evening with the sun almost hidden behind the clouds. I saw John's car from a distance and I could see there was also somebody in the passenger seat. The sun was blinding me as I kept on watching and the car was coming my direction. The closer they came my eyes started to get dizzy. The car pulled in and I could see for myself now who was in the passenger seat — Ronnie with a big smiling face as well.

I welcomed them in and they met my parents. Something inside me told me they hadn't come just to tell me they had no funding. After a while we got talking and John suddenly told me they got the money for Teamwork and that they were starting straight away on Monday 29 September. John also told me I had a job and then Ronnie broke in to say 'Bright and early Monday.' But I let it in one ear and out the other. Then Ronnie saw I wasn't responding to her talking. She then asked me was I coming back. I thought for a few moments and kept silent. Inside I felt like a dummy. Eventually I had to speak to her and answer no. I wasn't going back. In spite of my own heart I had to answer no.

But I knew with full heart I wanted that job more than anything else in this world. It meant heaven to me being with the group of young Travellers. I then realised I really said no. But yet I felt it couldn't be me saying no, when I wanted the job. At that moment I thought there was a tape recorder speaking those awful words to John and Ronnie. After a while both of them asked me was I sure I didn't want my job back. They also knew we had home problems. My parents were very strict on the family and the truth was I wasn't allowed take my job back for personal reasons.

John and Ronnie got up to go and I could feel my heart breaking inside me as they left saying goodbye. That evening I didn't want anyone next or near me, all I wanted was to be left alone so that I could think through for myself. I was thinking about the group again also John and Ronnie and wondered if ever I'd get the chance again to be a member of their group. But I can still remember I got no further as the tears flowed down my cheeks and wet my lips. The tears were like the rain coming from the sky.

The pain was really coming from my heart. I felt like a person who was getting ten years in prison for committing a crime. Through the painful hours I cried myself to sleep. The hours that night were like days to me as I lay half awake and went back to sleep again until something very loud in my head kept repeating 'Bright and early Monday.' Those words awoke me fully and I thought, 'That's what Ronnie mentioned to me earlier on in the day.' I was dreaming, dreaming of Ronnie's words haunting back to me. I sat up in bed and looked around me. I reached the window and looked out through it and tried to look at the sky. The colour of the sky had changed since I had fallen asleep. The frost on the window faded as I tried to wipe it with my hands so I could have a clear look up to the sky. I felt like everything was dead except me.

I couldn't help getting closer to the window to have a better view of the sky. It was a colour I couldn't describe with a full moon shining light towards me. I felt really safe again because the moon was protecting me. My eyes started to get weaker and weaker as I constantly kept on looking at the moon and felt the moon come closer and closer to me. One day I wished I would be taken from my sleep and wake up in the moon then that way I could go a lot of places around the world and see people I liked from high up in the sky. The moon then started to go back further and further in the clouds until I couldn't see anything.

The night passed on and yet I was awake in the same position as I was in an hour beforehand looking out the frosty glass window. I didn't remember much more after that until the next morning.

My head was laying near the window and my legs were wrapped under me trying to protect me from the cold. My head was feeling sore with pain. That morning I wasn't able to move, my whole body was numb. I couldn't talk or eat, all I wanted was to be left alone to think. To think about what was happening to me. I was feeling sick inside from not eating. I was alone that day and a lot more days that followed until I finally got things going. Maybe the things I was thinking were only dreams I was having. Maybe I just had to go somewhere I could have fun and sport or any entertainment. But there

121

was none of that available especially for Travellers like myself. My place was at home all day alone in a trailer with nothing to occupy my mind. Slowly but surely my heart-breaking pain started to ease a bit. I was getting over it. After some weeks I was able to go out on the streets begging.

This was my one and only chance to get away from home for a few hours each day, but I had to be home for a certain time. That's when I first became strongly involved in street begging. The following month of October was a cold and frosty one as I got up every morning early to get ready for begging and walked into town or sometimes I got a bus.

Sitting on the streets made my body tremble from the cold. I couldn't help myself from shaking as I would try to wrap my clothes tighter near my body to protect me from the frost and cold. My legs were always the worst part of me. When I would try to get up I just fell back down again. My legs were barely able to keep me standing firm.

As the months passed the weather started to get worse. Then the snow came. But the snow wasn't going to keep me from town because I had nothing else to do. I would sit on the snow with a piece of cardboard underneath me to stop the snow from getting at my clothes so they wouldn't get wet. The cardboard wasn't much help because if a policeman came along he would take it from me and throw it somewhere I wouldn't be able to get it. That left me sitting on the cold bare ground with the snow still underneath my body. I would go back to the same place when the police were out of sight.

Weeks passed and turned into months and I was still on the streets begging from ten in the morning until about three in the afternoon. There wasn't much more to look forward to but go home to my family. This begging was becoming a habit of mine. But then my health started to get worse as I got infections in my kidneys, ears and other parts of my body.

I also met Travellers my own age on the streets and also younger kids. The youngest I saw was about eight or nine years old. We quickly got to know one another. It didn't make any difference to me what age they were. We were all Travellers and that's all that mattered really. The children weren't from the inner city. They were from outside Dublin. I didn't know them very well and like I said we were the same as if we'd known each other for years as soon as we got talking. Those children were long begging on the streets before I even started. Therefore they had more experience of town than I had. Meeting every day with the group of young Travellers became a regular thing for me.

We would meet some mornings and chat about something that might have happened at home or something that would come off the top of our heads.

That conversation went on for a good half hour and we then separated and started to beg. Then when we would have money got, all of us ran into one another again. So this time it was time to count our money and get something to eat if we felt hungry — eating it on the street of course because Travellers are not allowed into most restaurants in town. We were mostly a group which had nothing else better to do with our own time, just mess and laugh all day.

Some days through those months all the group might be in a good mood for messing all the time. We would do things like phoning up the police, ambulance and fire brigade, telling them they were needed immediately, telling them that someone had thrown themselves into the Liffey or that they were needed at a certain place and we would be there waiting for them to come. When the ambulance arrived that's when the laughing took place as we watched the people looking in the Liffey for dead bodies. We would mostly do things we would get sport out of. We would also play games in town, games like running in and out of shops all day. That's where you have the confusion because the people would think you were going to ransack the place.

Unfortunately one day it didn't turn out happy for me. One of the shop-keepers held me until the police came. The shop-keeper then handed me over to the police who caught me and shoved me in the back of the van. Two policemen got in with me in case I might open the doors from the inside to jump out and get away from them. But that wasn't the only reason why they got in with me, it was so that they could give me a few clouts, kicks and pull my hair until I started to scream. But screaming didn't help me. The more I cried the more impatient the police got with me.

But yet in the van I was thinking of what I was going to go through in the station. Firstly I was pushed into a private department, put sitting down and I was asked to give my name, age and address. Then I was called for a search. On that occasion I was wearing my earrings and also I had about seven pounds in silver from begging. They took the money and earrings from me and started to bend my earrings which I had paid a big amount of money for. They asked me where I got them and how much I paid for them or if I had a receipt for them. Of course they were saying they were robbed, just because I was wearing them around town with me.

When I tried to stand up to ask for my money and earrings back I was given a shove and told to shut-up by a six-foot tall guy. I felt that he really hated me. The policeman then started to call me names like knacker, smelly, scumbag. Those names really made my blood boil. But I knew I couldn't say anything to him. My friends had warned me if I was ever in any incident with the police never to give them cheek or it would be worse for me because they would be harder on me in the cell. I tried hard to keep cool but yet I shouted and yelled at them whenever I got really angry.

They kept on questioning me and making a laugh of me until I was in the cell. They then told me to take off my coat and hand it to them. They walked out then and told me I could freeze if I wanted to. I can't tell you how bad the cells are with smell and just a bare concrete bed and one grey blanket thrown over it.

I was in that cell for about an hour and a half without anything to eat or drink. The policeman then came in with my charge sheet so then I could read what they were bringing me to court for. He also told me that he was waiting for transport to take me to court and after that he left.

Being in the cell for that length of time was really driving me nuts. I was praying for the transport to come and get me out of the station so I could see someone, at least I would take my breath for the short time I would be out in the fresh air.

Eventually the transport arrived and the policeman opened the cell door. He told me to get up on my feet which I did because I had no other choice. I walked to the door and as soon as I did he hit me on the head with the bunch of keys he had in his hand. I really felt it at that time. I tried to put my hands to my head but all he wanted me to do was keep moving until I was put into a police car.

We drove away, our next stop was court. I also had a bit of hassle from them on the way down. We landed there sharp and early and again the police had me by the shoulder. Of course the policemen knew the other policemen outside the court and I had four or five policemen laughing at me while I was being held. Everyone's eyes were on me. All I wished was that the ground would open so I could disappear. I never in my life felt so frightened as I was going into that court. The policeman then brought me down a long stairs and locked me up again inside iron bars like a monkey in the zoo. I was there for about twenty minutes. I was feeling weak. I didn't know what to think about any more behind the iron bars. One thing for sure I knew I was hungry. I never felt as hungry in my natural life because I hadn't eaten all day.

124

I heard my name being called from the top of the stairs. The policeman opened the gate and he brought me up the same stairs again but I wondered as I was going up would I be brought back down again if I got time in prison. The policeman told me beforehand what I had to do when I got in front of the judge.

When landed in front of the judge my heart was beating very fast and my legs were barely able to keep me up from the hunger and fear. In front of me was a mike so I had to stand to reach it. When the judge spoke to me he asked me a few questions and I felt that I had to answer them. It was just me alone in front of the judge with a policeman against me. In the court I was put on six months' probation. If I was ever caught again I would go to Mountjoy for a week's holiday and I would also pay a fine of £10.

I can't tell you how relieved I was when I heard those words coming out of his mouth. I was brought to sign the probation so after that I was as free as a bird, my wish to keep away from all sorts of people who make the laws, especially the policeman who had locked me up.

I left the court at about 2.30. The next step was to get something to eat but I had no money nor my bus fare home. I went back up to town and got a box and started to beg again. I waited on the street about two hours and still without anything to eat. I wasn't getting much money because I was too busy thinking about what had happened to me in the station. But while I was thinking the money started coming in. I had about six pounds again in my pocket so I thought I would get something to eat and then go home.

I went home and told my story but my parents didn't believe me at first about what had happened. I showed them my charge sheet and they got my younger sister to read it for them and then they believed me. That night went fairly quickly for me still thinking what they did to me. I was more determined than ever to make sure they didn't control me. All the police in Dublin weren't going to keep me from begging on the streets. I didn't mind if they beat me stupid this time, I was going to town the following day.

Next morning I was feeling a bit dizzy but it wasn't going to keep me back. I got my jacket and away I went. I went up to where I called my own begging spot and sat down and started collecting money. I was a few hours there and I saw some of my friends and we started talking.

I told them what had happened to me in the station. They weren't in town when I was caught as they were off somewhere else at the time so they didn't know anything about it. Of course they weren't surprised because it had happened them lots of times before.

I feel police could stop the begging on the street but all they ever think of is getting us shifted or locked up. Sometimes we got fun out of getting locked up if we had an easy time. It was like a bit of entertainment for us.

On the streets the police aren't the only problem for us Travellers. We also get a lot of hassle from the biggest majority of settled people. Like names thrown at us. We are also told things like 'You have no need to be sitting on the street, get a nice job for yourself.' But I explained to them people a hundred and one times, there are no jobs available, and there is no way a Traveller is going to get a job. Sitting on the street begging was, for me and the other young Travellers, a way to pass time because we had nothing else for doing.

I know how it must feel for settled poeple looking at us young Travellers on the streets. I get the impression that every time they saw us begging they think we had no food at home. Sometimes that was true. But from my point of view that isn't the main cause of young Travellers begging on the streets. In Ireland there is not much entertainment for young Travellers either at home or at school.

I know that the young children should be in school. I myself as a Traveller also felt for these children on the streets who can't write their own names. I believe that first the parents should be contacted and threatened. I also think that in Travellers' schools there is not enough in the school to keep the children interested. For the ones my own age I would like to see training centres for them. Something that will make them interested and have them look forward to something every morning they get up even if it's only for a short period of time. I would feel they would lose interest on the streets and realise that there is more to life than just sitting on the street every day. They are intelligent people. I feel the sooner the young Travellers get off the streets the better for themselves and other young people who might take the habit from them like I did.

I myself felt ashamed being on the streets begging, especially when all those people were looking at me from top to bottom. All I wanted to do was hide and try to turn away. Just sitting there on the streets made me feel dirty and unwanted by people.

Right now I am happy. I am working with a group of young Travellers on a Teamwork scheme for twelve months and I really feel I am wanted in life.

John and Ronnie are also here with us. I would love if those children on the streets were half as happy as me. Someday I hope they will be and become involved in something the same as I am. Being a member of a project makes you feel wanted. That's the way I feel at the moment. I am really learning something out of it for my own good and for others.

I would hate to think of myself going back to the streets again. I just hope I won't and I am trying very hard. If I hadn't this job I would be still on the streets messing and trying to make a fool of myself.

I feel there's a lot more to life now than just begging on the street if you will only get the opportunity to do it.

by Margaret Maughan

# Exchange House

Towards the end of 1979 and at the beginning of 1980 a group of mainly teenage Travelling young people were sleeping rough, sniffing glue and involved in petty crime in the city centre of Dublin. There were approximately forty young people in the gang, mainly between the ages of twelve and sixteen, with an equal number of boys and girls. The problem got extensive media coverage and there was considerable pressure on the Eastern Health Board to take action. Because of its involvement with the families of these young people through its alcoholic counsellor, social worker, youth workers and special residential home for Travellers, the Dublin Committee for Travelling People was offered funding by the health board to establish a pilot project to cater for the needs of these young people. Thus Exchange House was established in May 1980.

### THE YOUNG PEOPLE
Before 1980 a small number of Travelling families living near the city centre were identified by social workers as multi-problem families. The young people then sleeping rough were almost exclusively children of these families. In many cases there were fit persons orders on these young people, which orders were effectively unenforceable. The problems in the families ranged from excessive alcohol abuse to violence and serious neglect of the children. Given the conditions under which they lived and the large number of children in each family it was obvious that the situation would rapidly deteriorate. Sadly, the young children had from an early age been taught to beg. In many cases they later developed the habit of petty crime on the streets. Because

127

of the absence of any reasonable level of care at home these children grew into teenagers who had developed an ability to live and survive on the streets. Their sole source of emotional and social support was the gang of which they were all members. The gang provided material support in the form of money being equally shared. In addition and very importantly the gang provided protection from attack, and the girls, being particularly vulnerable, formed a gang within the gang to ensure that they remained safe from the special hazards for them of sleeping rough.

At the time the social workers of the statutory agencies found it impossible to work with these families. They had in effect become almost totally marginalised, bordering on being outside society. Their children were living on the streets, outside the law to all intents and purposes, and receiving none of the benefits or services which citizenship guarantees to our young people. In effect, the system had completely broken down for these young people. Society suffered, but most of all they themselves suffered in every possible way. These young people were set on a path of self-destruction, not only from the risk of accidents which goes with such a lifestyle, but more seriously from the intoxicants which they were inhaling (mainly glue) and the alcohol which they were constantly drinking.

### EXCHANGE HOUSE OPENS
It was against this background that Exchange House opened. Some of the staff knew the young people but the type of situation was new to us all and at first we were totally unaware of the complexities of the problems we were facing.

Initially, we approached the parents of the young people. They were quite happy for us to provide their children with shelter, and of course the house remained open to them to visit also. We then set about the task as we perceived it.

Night shelter seemed the obvious need, and after an initial period of openings and closures we were able to establish a night shelter facility. The closures were always occasioned by violence. The level of aggression was extremely high and to establish even the most basic rules was extremely difficult. The major problem we had to contend with was glue-sniffing. The glue made the young people very aggressive and violent and it seemed as if they were actually physically addicted to it.

We then opened a youth club in the afternoon (4.00 pm) which closed at 10.00 pm when the night shelter opened. Meals were provided in the youth club, as was television and various activities such as pool, juke box and table football. Although the youngsters came for the food, we found it impossible to compete with the glue, and most of the time the young people sat on the steps of the house sniffing glue as we helplessly looked on.

About the same time we undertook a very ambitious training/educational programme by day (between closure of the night shelter at 9.30 am and the opening of the youth club at 4.00 pm). This included carpentry, pottery, hairdressing, basket-making, numeracy and literacy. This project was ill-timed, as the excitement of the street (with everything from car chases by the police to going to court or hospital) was much more attractive.

For the first three years approximately, we seemed to be battling continually with the glue-sniffing. While we constantly attended the courts, hospitals, garda stations, with the young people, their self-destructive lifestyle seemed to continue regardless. However, towards the end of 1983 the use of the night shelter had almost completely disappeared, and by July 1984 we were able to redeploy all our staff during the day and evening time, providing emergency night shelter cover when necessary.

As the occurrence of young people sleeping rough decreased, the focus switched very much to the day time. Most of the same young people were now hanging around during the days and evenings and a new approach was called for. In addition, the level of aggression had considerably decreased. In 1982 we began work programmes for the fathers and older members of these families. These incorporated woodwork, copper and brass work, car mechanical work and some basic types of construction work. Now, however, the demand was coming from the young people for occupation. What had failed once now seemed to have a chance of getting going.

Our response was to establish two specialised work programmes, one for the boys and one for the girls. These are still operational and we feel have made a considerable contribution to giving self-respect, a sense of purpose and a sense of hope to our young people. The general lifestyle among the young people on the work programmes is almost identical to their Traveller counterparts attending training centres around the country. We also established a drop-in centre for those either not interested in work or for whom a job was not available and continued with a youth club service currently running four nights each week.

**THE NEEDS OF YOUNG PEOPLE OUT-OF-HOME**
Needs vary from individual to individual and from time to time. Needs

must always be assessed on an individual basis keeping in mind that the individual's needs are subject to change on a continuous basis.

Assessing the needs of the young people should not be done outside the context of their families. The needs of both are interdependent and equally important.

When Exchange House opened, the needs of the young people seemed very basic — shelter, food, clothing and medical care. These needs, once satisfied, were replaced immediately with new ones, much more difficult to satisfy. Among these were security, care, discipline and self-respect. By providing a caring and consistent service many such needs were met at least partly.

It was important to involve ourselves in the lives of the young people only where and when it was necessary. If somebody could go home at night we did not provide night shelter for him or her. Working with the families (especially the parents) was part of our strategy. Fathers working, for example, help greatly in this respect and we reached the stage when making demands on the families seemed appropriate.

Our objective where possible was to facilitate the re-establishment of the extended family support system which is the traditional and proven way Travelling people cope with excessive demands on parents by large families. The second objective was to facilitate the re-establishment of these families as self-respecting and respected members of the broader Travelling community.

**THE PRESENT SERVICE PROVISION OF EXCHANGE HOUSE**

WORK PROGRAMMES
Exchange House runs in effect seven different programmes with anywhere between twenty-six and thirty-four Travelling people employed at any given time. Five of the programmes are for men and are as follows:

- A scrap yard to which scrapped cars are brought from the Travellers' sites around the city, thus improving the public image of Travelling people. They are stripped in the yard and then sold

- Two teams of men who renovate properties, paint houses, construct extensions to houses

- A copper and brass craft workshop

- A rug-making programme

The last two of the above are based inside the house, while the others are outside.

We also, as already mentioned, run a work programme for girls and one for boys within the house. These incorporate numeracy and literacy classes, life-skills classes and some outings. All the boys and girls are over fifteen and under twenty. Where appropriate we transfer the young boys to one of the more work-orientated programmes, thus making room for someone new to come in.

## WOMEN'S CLUB

The club at the moment takes place once each week, is aimed particularly at young mothers and incorporates a creche facility. It enables us to work more closely with the mothers, giving them a little space for themselves and in many cases the only break they may have in the whole week.

## EMERGENCY NIGHT SHELTER

Where need for emergency night shelter now arises we organise the accom-modation and endeavour to sort out the long-term situation as soon as possible. This need only now arises very infrequently.

## YOUTH CLUB

We run the youth club on four evenings each week. The club incorporates pool, table-tennis, table football, space invaders, a very basic gym (equipped by the young people themselves) and a shop. In addition, we have a swimming outing and a football game once each week.

The youth work programme (in this specialised context) contributes in many ways as much to the development of the young people as do the more formal classes incorporated in the work programmes. Through the various activities the young people are informally educated and, more importantly, develop their ability to socialise.

In addition, the youth club provides a very important point of contact with any of the young people who may be sniffing glue or sleeping rough.

The average youth club attendance is ten. It is very well attended during the winter period with a large falling off in the summer months.

## DROP-IN CENTRE

The drop-in centre is exactly that. A cup of tea and somewhere to sit down in a warm atmosphere is available. So too is a pool table in a separate room which is constantly in use.

Here, young people not on the work programmes can obtain casual work where a place on the more structured work programmes is either unavailable or inappropriate.

In addition to pool, darts, table-football and board games are often played. The drop-in centre serves as a second youth club in this sense and the organisation of this part of its role is almost entirely done by the young Travellers now.

Problems constantly present themselves. The drop-in staff either deal with the crisis themselves where Exchange House is involved with the people concerned, or alternatively refer to the appropriate outside agency, for example, Dublin Corporation social workers/Eastern Health Board social workers.

The drop-in centre has always been the scene of much socialising among the inner city families particularly, but also enables them to mix with other Travellers from the outskirts of the city. This is extremely important as the multi-problem families are a very isolated group, even within the Travelling community.

In addition it enables the staff, the other members of the settled community who frequent the house and the Travelling people to socialise with one another in a relaxed atmosphere.

The staff of the drop-in centre also monitor the situation vis-à-vis new outbreaks of glue-sniffing, drinking, sleeping rough. This is done through the contact with Centre Care, Focus-Point, the Simon community, and through walks around the sites and the streets of the city centre.

The average daily attendance in the drop-in centre is thirty. This does not include young children or casual callers.

SOCIAL WORK
Our social work service is the umbrella service for all the others I have mentioned.

The young people on the work programmes are cared for while they are on the work programmes by their supervisors. If they are sniffing glue and on the streets they will get the attention of our drop-in staff and perhaps our youth worker. When the other services can effectively satisfy the need the social work service merely co-ordinates and supervises the involvement of the other services. However, whenever they go outside the scope of these services the social work service gets directly involved. Examples of this are when the young people are in prison, court, hospital or when they have run away from home, down the country, for example.

More importantly we also provide a social work service to the multi-problem families which has developed very successfully since the very difficult days when the house first opened.

SUMMARY
These services provided by Exchange House cannot be assessed individually. They are all part of a co-ordinated response to the plight of multi-problem Travelling families. The strength and value of the programme lie in the co-ordination of these services and the degree to which they complement one another. In addition, while our initial brief was to work with the young people at risk, we have developed a powerful and very effective family support system. Through experience we have learned that this is the only long-term approach likely to deal successfully with the problems we encounter. The employment of a father in one of the work programmes for example can be the crucial factor in stabilising his whole family situation. Attending the women's club can make the lives of some of the mothers that vital bit more tolerable to the benefit of the entire family. A problem spotted in the drop-in centre can be easily dealt with when noticed early enough. And so it goes on. If one aspect were to be emphasised it would be the nature and strength of the relationship with the Travelling people. Being close to the scene and in a position to act without delay when problems arise is crucial. It is difficult to envisage the situation we encountered in 1980 ever developing again. Proven preventative measures can now be taken should such problems arise again.

On our own, Exchange House would not be able adequately to tackle the problems we encounter. St Columba's day care centre (for the younger children of the multi-problem families) and the residential homes at New-townmountkennedy and Roundwood complete the overall family support service. While the roles of Trudder House and Derralossary are clearly definable, ours must, as the back-up service for all three, be very much a multi-purpose one. They could not operate without such a back-up service, nor could we make much significant progress without the specialised and complementary services provided by the other three.

**OTHER NEEDS**

SERVICES
The initial problem we faced was that the services that are available to the public at large were not being received by the families with whom we work.

There is often a tendency to set up a new service when the need is to adapt those services already in existence to the needs of different groups. For example, the children of multi-problem families can avail of primary education and training in junior training centres if the pupil/teacher or trainee/instructor ratio is reduced. The ratio of social workers to families should of course also be considerably less than average to ensure that the work can be done properly.

The service that appears to be completely underestimated in terms of its potential contribution to the needs of young people out-of-home is a properly co-ordinated youth service. We find our youth club an invaluable support service for the rest of the work. There is no doubt that such clubs for deprived sections of the community are extremely beneficial in so many ways.

ACTIVITIES

Activities are extremely important where boredom and a sense of purposelessness and worthlessness are fundamental problems. For the Travelling people we work with, it was crucial to break the sense of helplessness which had become pervasive. Through employment in productive jobs and involvement in leisure-time activities the ice can be broken and once a progressive pattern is established people take more and more responsibility for their lives and regain their self-respect.

TRAINING

One of the great strengths of the Travelling people is their ability to learn anything that is functional, though they have little interest in anything purely academic. On this basis training must always be directly relevant to the lives the people lead and their traditional occupations. The training should never create dependency but rather should make a lasting contribution to the lives of the trainees.

CO-ORDINATION AND POLICY

Co-ordination is a major problem. There are many services established on a haphazard basis. While all of the various agencies involved are extremely busy and often overwhelmed by the work-load there is not a general awareness of the services provided by other agencies. This contributes to a waste of resources and after a while the quality of the services deteriorates. In addition, services are very prone to adopting new roles when finding difficulty in serving their original function. Constant contact among the agencies would greatly economise in resources and facilitate the extension of services; it would also result in an improvement in the services already being provided.

As a general observation it would certainly seem that any response to crisis situations should be made within the framework of a broader-ranging policy. Such a policy should be based on detailed research with a view to assessing needs which have not been expressed, distinguishing between demands and needs and monitoring the changes in needs as they occur. Again, a great deal of harm can be done by responding inappropriately to a situation because of mistaken perception of the needs.

PROVISION OF SERVICES

In our experience the provision of services, activities, training, co-ordination and policy came through one agency initially, ie Exchange House (Dublin Committee for Travelling People). This proved extremely advantageous as relevant information and experience were passed on between people involved in the different services against the background of a constantly changing scene. In the light of experience, given the serious situation that existed it would appear that one agency being involved was preferable. In terms of funding, the Exchange House project was funded by the Eastern Health Board. The work programmes were funded by the Youth Employment Agency with the Vocational Education Committee funding the educational input. In addition, the work programmes have received contract work on a continuous basis from Dublin County Council and Dublin Corporation towards improving the environment in which Travelling people around the city live. Involving Travelling people in such work is certainly a step in the right direction.

As the situation has improved other agencies have become more involved and it would seem that once the crisis situation has been dealt with and preventative work has been started, slowly but surely the families and young people with whom we worked could more and more avail of general services available to Travelling people. While co-ordination and co-operation are still extremely important the work can then be done by the various agencies as normal.

by John O'Brien

# Young People Out-of-Home and the Law

Under the Children's Act 1908, as amended, a child is defined as aged between seven and fifteen, and a young person as aged between fifteen and seventeen years. Under the Age of Majority Act 1984 a young person now becomes an adult at the age of eighteen years.

## WHEN CAN A YOUNG PERSON LEAVE HOME?

The Guardianship of Infants Act 1964, as amended, provides for parents having jurisdiction and guardianship rights over their children up to the age of eighteen generally. A young person cannot acquire an independent domicile until he or she reaches the age of eighteen.

However, at common law, a boy was said to reach the age of 'discretion' at fourteen and a girl at the age of sixteen. The age of 'discretion' was regarded as the age at which the person reached a certain level of maturity and could decide, for example in custody disputes, which parent they wanted to live with.

A person can contract a lawful marriage if they are of the age of sixteen.

It would be helpful if there was a clear statutory provision indicating at what age children can leave home, without parental consent.

## POLICE INTERVENTION

Generally the Garda HQ would take the view that anyone under the age of eighteen should be returned home if they are reported as missing. A description of a missing person is circulated by the teleprinter to every garda station. The gardaí state that there are approximately 1100 persons missing altogether, but they do not keep separate statistics in relation to the ages of those missing. By the end of the year there would be approximately only forty still regarded as untraced.

There are certain archaic criminal offences that seek to punish those who assist young persons to leave home. The first of these is section 56 of the Offences Against the Person Act 1861, which provides that it is an offence

136

for anyone to take away, entice or detain, by force or by fraud, any young person under the age of fourteen, 'with intent to deprive any parent, guardian, or other person having the lawful care or charge of such child, of the possession of such child'. It is also an offence to receive or harbour a young person who has been removed under these circumstances. However, prosecutions are unlikely, as those offences imply *deliberate* unlawful acts.

There was a case heard in the supreme court in 1943 called The People' (A.G.) *v* Edge (1943 Irish Reports, p. 115), which dealt with an alleged kidnapping. The court held that the defendant could not be convicted of kidnapping, after he had taken a fourteen-year-old boy away from his parents with the boy's consent, but without parental consent. The court indicated that the boy was of sufficient age and intelligence to give a real consent. However, if the boy had been below the age of discretion, he would have been regarded as incapable of giving consent, and the crime of false imprisonment would have been committed.

## PARENTAL INTERVENTION TO SEEK THE RETURN OF A CHILD OR YOUNG PERSON

The civil law has another archaic action, which could theoretically be used against someone encouraging a child away from home. The rationale of this law is that a father, as purported head of the house, has a legal right to the services of his unmarried children who ordinarily live at home. This action for 'loss of services' arose out of a similar right that a man had over his wife. However, those actions (of criminal conversation, harbouring and enticement of a spouse) were abolished in the Family Law Act 1981.

The legal basis of this action is the loss of services, and not the parental relationship itself. If a child is too young to give any services, or is in the service of another, and not living with his or her parents, a parent cannot obtain damages. In such an action the court cannot order the return of the child but can grant an injunction to restrain harbouring or otherwise depriving a parent of the child's services, and give damages. Damages are not confined to the financial worth of the services lost, but as compensation for the damage done to the pride and honour of the parents. There was a case in England called Lough *v* Ward 1945 (AER 338) in which an action was taken where a young girl entered a religious society without parental consent.

## HABEAS CORPUS

Parents could seek to obtain a conditional order of *habeas corpus* (ie produce the body) against an agency who they think has information on a missing child, or where they clearly seek the return of the child and the agency has refused to return the child. The high court would order the agency to pro-

137

duce the child or young person in court, and show why they wish to continue to hold on to him or her. In effect, it would become a hearing as to who got custody. But in the case of A.G. *v* Edge the judge indicated that 'if however the minor has a view of his own, and the Court finds that he is no longer a mere child, but is capable of consenting, or not consenting, to the place where he is detained, and in fact consents, then the ground for *habeas corpus* falls away'.

### WARDSHIP

Parents can try and get their child made a ward of court by taking high court proceedings. For example, this can be used to prevent a young person leaving home, especially where the young person is likely to go and live with a boy- or girl-friend that the parents disapprove of. Wardship has also been used where a child has gone to live with relatives and the parents are seeking the child's return. In those cases, indeed, the relatives can make the child a ward of court, as they do not have, strictly, the power to issue proceedings under the Guardianship of Infants Act 1964. Recently the wardship jurisdiction has been used by the Eastern Health Board, in cases of young girls aged sixteen to eighteen who have been sexually abused, where the 'fit person procedure', which deals with those under sixteen, could not be used.

Finally, the parents could seek a general equitable injunction to order the agency to return the young person back to their physical custody.

### THE CONSTITUTIONAL POSITION

The constitution can be used by parents to assert their rights *vis-à-vis* a child or young person. While the family based on marriage is given strong constitutional protection, by article 41, children and young persons are not so clearly protected. Some of the rights of a child (and presumably a young person would be included in that definition) were set out in an adoption case called G. *v* An Bord Uchtála 1980 (IR Reports, p. 32) where Chief Justice O'Higgins stated 'the child also has natural rights . . . Having been born, the child has the right to be fed and to live, to be reared and educated, to have the opportunity of working and of realising his or her full personality and dignity as a human being. These rights of the child (and others which I have not enumerated) must equally be protected and vindicated by the State.'

Children belonging to a family based on marriage have the additional right that the state is supposed to protect the family to which he or she belongs (article 41.2), the right to be educated by the family and to be provided by his or her parents with religious, moral, intellectual, physical and social education (article 42.1).

Article 42.5 sets out when the state can intervene in the lives of children: 'in exceptional cases, where the parents, for physical or moral reasons fail in their duty towards their children, the State, as Guardian of the common good, by appropriate means shall endeavour to supply the place of the parents, but always with due regard for the natural and imprescriptible rights of the child'. This article was interpreted in the controversial case of McC. and M.C. *v* K.C. and A.C. and An Bord Uchtála and An Ard Cláraitheoir (unreported judgement of 27 March 1985). This case was an adoption case, but it gave the supreme court the opportunity of setting out its views in relation to children and families and intervention.

The judge said that the state cannot supplant the rule of parents in providing for the infant the rights to be educated conferred on it by article 42.1, except 'in exceptional cases' arising from a failure, for moral or physical reasons, to provide that education. He went on to say that section 3 of the Guardianship of Infants Act 1964 (which is the act dealing with disputes over custody of children) must be construed as involving a constitutional presumption that the welfare of the child is to be found within the family, unless the court is satisfied on the evidence that there are *compelling reasons* why this cannot be achieved.

This case is important, because it has been interpreted as meaning that in the case of a conflict between parental and children's rights the parents' rights would prevail. It has also influenced the Department of Health in their redrafting of the Children's (Care and Protection) Bill 1985, in setting out the powers that health boards will have in taking children or young persons away from parents.

### YOUNG PEOPLE AND THE VAGRANCY ACTS
Section 4 of the Vagrancy Act 1824 is still in force and it provides that 'every person wandering abroad and lodging in any barn or out house, or in any cart or wagon, not having a visible means of subsistence, and not giving a good account of himself or herself . . . shall be deemed a rogue and vagabond and shall be guilty of an offence, punishable by three months imprisonment.' The sort of young person that comes into this category is lumped into the same section with those who are up for indecent exposure, persons pretending to tell fortunes, persons having offensive weapons, etc. However, the Garda Siochána guide (which is regarded as the standard textbook for gardaí on this section) indicates that the gardaí do not have the power to arrest for the said offences, as the provisions giving power of arrest were not extended by the British act to Ireland.

Section 3 of the Vagrancy (Ireland) Act 1847 provides for a penalty of one month's imprisonment for any person wandering abroad and begging, or placing himself in any public place, street, highway, port or passage to beg or gather alms, or causing or procuring or encouraging any child or children so to do. Section 14 of the Children's Act 1908 provided for a penalty of three months' imprisonment or a fine of £25 for any person causing a child or young person to beg. Section 84 of the Children's (Care and Protection) Bill 1985 provides for the continuation of that section but increases the penalty to six months' imprisonment or a fine of £500. Section 85 of the new Children's Bill gives the gardaí a power of arrest if they suspect that the person will abscond for the purposes of evading justice or will obstruct justice. The gardaí, however, under section 86 of the new bill, would be obliged to notify the health board if they do summons that person.

## ASSISTING YOUNG PEOPLE OUT-OF-HOME
No one is obliged in law to return young people to the police or their parents. Police have no power to be admitted into a premises, generally speaking, unless they have a search warrant. However, there are certain offences that could be committed, by assisting young persons who have run away from reformatories or prisons, and workers in this area should be aware of these. Section 72 of the 1908 Children's Act says that a young offender who escapes from a reformatory school can be punished by having his detention increased by six months, or if he is over seventeen, he can be imprisoned for three months. Sub-section 6 of that section provides that if any person knowingly assists or induces directly or indirectly an offender or child detained in, or placed out on licence from, a certified school to escape from the school, or from any person with whom he is placed on licence, or knowingly harbours, conceals or prevents from returning to school, or knowingly assists in so doing, commits a criminal offence and can receive a sentence of two months' imprisonment or £20 fine.

## RUNNING AWAY FROM CARE
Section 22 of the Children's Act 1908 provides that if anyone knowingly assists or induces, directly or indirectly, a child or young person to escape from the person to whose care he or she is committed, under part 2 of the act (ie in care under section 24/section 21) or knowingly harbours, conceals or prevents from returning to such person, a child or young person who has so escaped, or knowingly assists in so doing, can be sentenced to two months' imprisonment or a fine of £20. Section 51 of the Children's Bill 1985 will provide that a child who is in the care of the health board, who leaves that care without the consent of the board, may be returned to that care by an authorised officer of the health board or, at the request of the health board, by the gardaí. If someone obstructs or interferes with that, they can be sentenced to three months' or a fine of £350.

140

## CIVIL POWERS

If parents demand the return of a young person under the age of seventeen and there is no court order enforced and the staff at the hostel or agency feel that the young person is at risk of physical or sexual abuse, then the staff member can apply to the children's court for a place of safety order. The powers to do so are not confined to the health board. Ironically, a hostel could be regarded in law as a place of safety, as section 131 of the act defines the place of safety as 'any workhouse or police station or any Hospital, Surgery or any other suitable place, the occupier of which is willing temporarily to receive an infant child or young person'. The young person would then be detained at the place of safety until the fit person proceedings, issued under section 24, are heard. Section 24 is a section dealing with children or young persons who have been assaulted, ill-treated or neglected in a manner likely to cause them unnecessary suffering or to be injurious to their health.

Proceedings under section 58 could also be issued. The court then decides whether it is going to commit the child or young person to the care of the fit person. Section 38(1) of the 1908 act defines a 'fit person' as including any society or body corporate established for the reception or protection of poor children or the prevention of cruelty to children.

Section 58 of the act allows for certain classified children to be sent to industrial schools, which was a response of that time to abandoned and other children, though sub-section 7 provided that the court could commit the child to a relative or other fit person in lieu of the school. Section 58 covers a wide category of children, including those found begging, or receiving alms, or found not having any home or settled place of abode or visible means of subsistence, or having a parent or guardian who does not exercise proper guardianship, or found destitute and having his or her parents undergoing imprisonment or 'otherwise living in circumstances calculated to cause, encourage, or favour the seduction or prostitution of the child'.

Section 58, sub-section 8, provides that the police are under a duty to take the proceedings unless the case is one within the cognisance of the local education authority, or proceedings are being taken by another person, or the police authorities are satisfied that the taking of proceedings is undesirable in the interest of the child. Despite this law, the police seem to exercise a discretion now not to take proceedings, except if pressure is brought to bear on them, in relation to children begging (usually in the tourist season) or children acting as prostitutes. The health boards do not seem to have a clear statutory responsibility either.

The new Children's Bill will only allow the health boards to get care orders, though any person can continue to apply for a place of safety order. It will not be possible, therefore, for voluntary organisations to take these orders, if that bill comes into force, though admittedly they have not used the relevant sections of the 1908 act. This is not a criticism of those organisations, but just an example of how little known the law relating to children is. The judiciary have not supported any innovative use of the existing law. Indeed the Kennedy Report in 1970 commented on the fact that the fit person mechanism was not being used by parties other than the health board.

An agency could also seek an injunction against a parent who is constantly harassing a young person residing with them or staff members. They could apply to have a young person made a ward of court where the parents are demanding the young person back, particularly in a case where there is not sufficient evidence to go under fit person proceedings and where a young person is suffering from a mental or physical handicap. Wardship can be used to the age of eighteen in the case of a minor and at any age if a court feels the person is suffering from such a degree of mental infirmity that they are incapable of looking after themselves or their affairs.

### POSITION OF THE HEALTH BOARDS

Section 65 of the Health Act 1953 provides for assistance to certain bodies. The health authority may, with the approval of the minister, give assistance in any one or more of the following ways to any body which provides or proposes to provide a service, similar or ancillary to a service which the health authority may provide:

- by contributing to the expenses incurred by the body

- by supplying fuel, light, food, water or other commodity

- by permitting the use by the body of premises maintained by the health authority and, where requisite, executing alterations and repairs to, and supplying furniture and fittings for, such premises

- by providing premises (with all requisite furniture and fittings) for use by the body

Sub-section 2 provides that the health authority may, with ministerial approval, contribute to the funds of any society for the prevention of cruelty to children. This section remains in force, and the new Children's Bill does not propose to repeal it, as obviously it is not restricted to services provided for children. Indeed the new section 55 of the Children's Bill deals with the health board providing, equipping and maintaining any premises required

142

for the provision of services under that act. However, it allows sweeping powers to the health board to discontinue the provision and maintenance of any premises or any service, provided it gets ministerial consent. It also allows the minister to direct the health board, after consultation with it, to discontinue the provision and maintenance of any premises or any service, and the health board must comply with any such direction.

Section 56 of the new bill provides that the health board may, in accordance with such conditions as may be specified by the minister, make and carry out an arrangement with a person or body to provide services under the act.

Section 55 of the Health Act 1953 empowers the health board to have *a child* cared for by boarding him or her out, by sending him to a school approved by the Minister for Health, or, if over fifteen, placing him in employment or in a course for the learning of a trade, calling or business.

The health board may act in relation to any child who is eligible for 'institutional assistance' under section 54 of the act and who is a legitimate child whose parents are dead, or who is deserted by his or her parents or by a surviving parent, or an illegitimate child deserted by his or her mother.

Section 54, sub-section 2 provides that a person who is unable to provide *shelter* and maintenance for himself or his dependants, shall, for the purposes of this section, be eligible for institutional assistance. This is defined as meaning shelter and maintenance in a county home or similar institution. The 1953 act allowed for the boarding out of those under the age of sixteen, but the health board could continue to support the child after sixteen until 'the completion of the child's education'.

The new Children's Bill — in particular section 47 — provides that where a young person is in the care of a health board and attains the age of eighteen, the board may, if it is satisfied as to his or her need for assistance, continue to assist the young person as long as his or her welfare appears to require it and he or she has not attained the age of twenty-one. The health board may assist him or her by causing him to be visited or assisted, by arranging for the completion of his education, and by contributing towards his maintenance, while he is completing his education, by placing him in a suitable trade or *by arranging hostel or other forms of accommodation for him*. It also gives powers for the minister, with the consent of the Minister for Finance, to make regulations governing the provision of assistance under this section and such regulations may in particular provide for requiring persons to contribute in specified cases, towards the cost of providing them with accommodation.

143

The Minister for Education has jurisdiction over youthful offenders whose period of detention expires, and in theory, under section 68 of the 1908 act, they remain under the supervision of the managers of the schools until nineteen years. This can be extended until twenty-one, if the minister directs that it is necessary for the protection and welfare of the youthful offender.

The only other sections in the Children's Bill that are relevant to children who are out-of-home or that may be used implicitly to deal with them, are section 23, which provides that a health board is to promote the welfare of children as *far as practicable* in its area, by identifying children who are receiving, or are at risk of receiving, inadequate care and protection, and providing such advice, guidance, *services and facilities* as may diminish the need to receive such children into care or keep them in care.

Section 42 provides that the health board shall as far as practicable promote the welfare of children in its area and, in doing this, shall have regard to the principle that it is generally best that a child should be brought up in his or her own family. Where this is not possible the health board shall *provide him with such care as is most appropriate to his needs* and, before taking a decision, take into account the age of the child and have regard to the wishes of the child.

The Health Act 1970 established the health boards and provided that the functions previously performed by local authorities under the Health Acts of 1947, 1966, etc should now be performed by the boards. Section 25 of the 1970 act provided that where a local authority was of the opinion that it would be more convenient that any power, function or duty, which may be exercised or performed by it should be exercised or performed by a health board, and the health board is willing to do it, the authority and the board, with the consent of the Minister for Local Government, could make an arrangement for that power, function or duty to be so exercised or per-formed by the health board. Section 26 went on to provide that a health board may, in accordance with such conditions as may be specified by the minister, make and carry out an arrangement with a person or body to pro-vide services under the Health Acts of 1947 and 1970 for persons eligible for such services.

**YOUNG PERSONS OUT-OF-HOME AND HOUSING**
Section 12 of the Housing Act 1966 provided for the housing authority to give assistance to certain bodies who were going to deal with housing for elderly persons or who would provide dwellings, which would help to secure one of the primary objectives under section 60, sub-section 3. The latter

section dealt with houses which were unfit for human habitation, eliminating over-crowding, providing housing for persons (including elderly or disabled persons) who, in the opinion of the housing authority, are in need of and are unable to provide such accommodation from their own resources. There was nothing in the act that dealt clearly with the needs of the homeless. The Housing (Miscellaneous Provisions) Bill 1985 was brought in with a view to dealing with the needs of homeless persons. It is inadequate, and I would endorse the recommendations of Simon calling for changes in the bill. Section 2 of that bill regards as homeless someone who has no accommodation available which, in the opinion of the authority, he or she (together with any other person who normally resides with him or who might reasonably be expected to reside with nim) can reasonably occupy or remain in occupation of, or who is living in a night shelter or other such institution because he or she has no accommodation.

The bill has been criticised because it does not specifically list hostels and it does not deal with the situation of persons who have to leave home because of domestic violence. I would extend Simon's criticism: the bill does not cover the situation where young persons have to leave home because of physical or sexual abuse or neglect. The difficulty with the bill is that the duty to provide accommodation relates to 'a person regarded by the housing authority as being homeless and capable of living independently' (Section 10(1)(a)). This allows the authority to argue that young persons under the age of eighteen are *not* capable of living independently, so that would need to be amended.

The bill also provides that a person is not to be regarded as being homeless if the housing authority 'are of the opinion that he has deliberately or without good or sufficient reason done or failed to do anything, in consequence of which accommodation is not available for him which it would have been or would be, reasonable to occupy'. This gives far too much discretion to the housing authority who could take the view that a young person should, for example, try and obtain an injunction to put out the parent who is abusing them, rather than leaving home and expecting the housing authority to house them.

Section 10 indicates that the housing authority may, for the purposes of providing accommodation for homeless persons, make arrangements with a body for providing accommodation, or provide financial assistance, or where they are not otherwise able to fulfil that duty, may rent accommodation, arrange lodgings or contribute to the cost of such accommodation or lodgings. The housing authority may also require that person to pay towards the cost of such accommodation. However, as the Simon document criticising the bill

145

states 'local authorities could technically and legally comply with the Act by placing homeless persons in overcrowded bedsits or sub-standard lodgings'. This would be particularly serious in the case of vulnerable young persons who would have less coping abilities than adults. This is what has happened in England and we cannot allow that situation to develop here.

There is nothing in the Housing Bill which deals with the age of homeless persons and I think the bill should be amended to specifically cover their needs, where the health board is not in a position to cater for their needs.

### SUPPLEMENTARY WELFARE ALLOWANCE

A child dependant is defined under section 119 of the act as meaning, in relation to a recipient, any child, not being an adult dependant, who has not attained the age of eighteen years and who is dependent on that recipient for support. Section 214 sets out that parents are under a legal obligation to maintain their dependants under the age of sixteen years. The irony is that there is no provision under the Family Law (Maintenance of Spouses and Children) Act 1976 in which a child can bring proceedings against a parent, to force the parent to maintain him or her. However, the health board has the power, under section 215, to force the parent to contribute, by making an application to the district court.

Section 200 sets out clearly that every 'person' in the state whose means are insufficient to meet his or her needs and the needs of any adult or child dependent on him or her shall be entitled to supplementary welfare allowance. Section 209 indicates that if the supplementary welfare allowance is not sufficient to meet their needs, then the allowance may be increased. This is to cover rent allowance.

Section 211 provides for the health board, by reason of *exceptional circumstances*, to meet the needs of a person by goods and services. In the case of *sudden* and urgent need, the health board may dispense with inquiry before giving those goods or services.

Section 212 gives them power to make single payments for *exceptional* need and, finally, section 213 provides for payment to *anyone* in cases of *urgency*.

The whole appeal system, in relation to refusal to give supplementary welfare or any additional allowance, needs to be changed to give the applicant a proper appeal structure. The commission on social welfare report identified one of the problems in the scheme as being a lack of an agreed interpretation of the guide-lines for making discretionary payments and suggested that the whole supplementary welfare allowance scheme should be integrated into the social welfare system.

## JUDICIAL REVIEW

The high court has the power to review the orders of courts or tribunals where decisions are made in excess of jurisdiction, where natural or constitutional justice is ignored in the procedures, and where there is an error of law on the face of the order or decision. This is by granting an 'order of certiorari'. The high court also has the power to make an order prohibiting or restraining an administrative body from initiating or continuing an action which would usurp a jurisdiction or function, in excess of its statutory power. The high court can also grant an 'order of mandamus' to compel an administrative body to perform a function or legal duty which it is refusing to do. Judicial review has been used in the last few years by FLAC and Coolock Community Law Centre in the area of social welfare law. Where the health boards or the Department of Social Welfare fail to carry out their statutory duties or obligations, or do so in a manner which is not in accordance with natural or constitutional justice, the courts have power to intervene and insist on justice being done.

by Paula Scully

# Recommendations

The three main issues which caused grave concern to speakers and participants at the seminar were:

1 lack of adequate legislation concerning children and young people

2 lack of proper co-ordination, integrated administrative structures with regard to policy, planning and delivery of services for children and young people

3 lack of appropriate community and residential provision for children and young people especially those between twelve and eighteen years of age

Improvements were demanded in legislation, in administration, in research, in preventative and supportive work with families, in residential care, in accommodation and in youth services.

### LEGISLATION
1 There should be an amendment to the constitution which will clearly establish the paramount rights of children and young people.

2 The Children (Care and Protection) Bill should be amended so that care and protection may be provided for children and young people up to eighteen years of age.

3 A system of family courts should be established for all legal matters pertaining to children and young people.

4 Young people between the ages of sixteen and eighteen years of age who cannot remain in their own homes and are not in residential care should be provided with a guaranteed form of income maintenance under the Social Welfare Act.

### PREVENTATIVE AND SUPPORTIVE SERVICES FOR THE FAMILY
The seminar pointed out that the present statutory social work services were under-resourced and crisis-oriented rather than preventative and it made the following recommendations:

1 More family support services should be available to provide a wide range of supportive and preventative services for children and their families experiencing difficulties. These services could play a major role in preventing youth homelessness.

2 Services should be localised and accessible to families. Families with difficulties should know where to go to seek and receive help.

3 Family resource centres should be established to provide support for families and enable them to get through various crises in their lives. They should act in a preventative role so that young people and children are maintained within their own homes and within the community when at all possible.

4 There should be adequate aftercare for young people who have been reared in residential care to reintegrate them back into their own families and community. It was pointed out that young people who have been in care form a significant group of the homeless population.

## RESIDENTIAL CARE

1 Residential care services for young people should be provided in such a way that they are as close as possible to that which is normal in the culture and for the age and circumstances of the young people.

2 Residential care should be provided in all areas, so that young people can remain in contact with their own families. This is particularly important in high risk areas.

3 Residential care should be integrated into services in the local area so that young people can mix and make friends with those not in residential care.

4 Residential homes or hostels should be small and should provide for not more than ten young people.

5 Residential care and foster care services should be developed for all young people up to the age of eighteen who cannot remain in their own homes.

6 Residential care should be seen as part of a continuum of care services. There should be a wide range of residential services available to young people up to the age of eighteen years of age with differing needs. These should include a range of emergency care, short-term care, long-term and therapeutic care as well as assessment centres.

7 Where possible, in keeping with normalisation principles, those who need treatment or specialised services should receive these on an outpatient basis.

8 There should be residential therapeutic provision for those who are particularly disturbed and destructive. Again this should be part of a continuum of services, all of which should aim towards less specialised provision.

9 Priority should be given to make provision to meet the needs of young people who are substance users.

10 Recognition should be given to the fact that young people throughout the country need different forms of care. It is essential therefore that each health board should make provision for a wide range of services to meet the varying needs of young people within their region. At present there is no emergency accommodation for young boys in Cork, for young girls in Galway or for boys or girls in Limerick.

11 The purpose, objectives and activities of different residential settings should be clearly defined and known to those working within those residential settings and those outside of them. In that way duplication could be avoided and gaps in services could be more clearly identified and responded to.

12 Training and support for staff in different areas of children's services should be available as a priority.

**HOUSING**

1 The Housing (Miscellaneous Provisions) Bill 1985 should be amended and passed.

2 Local authorities should assume the responsibility for providing accommodation for young people over sixteen years of age. Priority should be given to young people leaving residential care and who cannot return to their own homes. Health board children's services should liaise with the local authority housing sections in making arrangements for this accommodation.

3 A range of accommodation options with varying degrees of support should be available to young people, such as semi-independent supportive accommodation, halfway houses, shared accommodation. These should be provided for young people who do not need residential or hostel accommodation but who are not capable of living independently.

**YOUTH SERVICES**

1 There is a need for a properly co-ordinated youth policy which would take into account policies and activities of the various statutory and voluntary agencies involved with and responsible for young people. This will ensure that education and intervention are planned properly and that the complementary roles of these agencies are maximised.

2  Local youth services should play a major role in the co-ordination of services for young people.

3  There is a need for a wide range of services at community level especially in areas where there is a high incidence of homeless children and young people. These include outreach work, drop-in centres, unstructured and structured youth clubs, day activity centres and training centres.

4  The existing health board statutory services are remote and inaccessible to young people. Some are remote geographically, others remote culturally. There is a need for a wide range of services at community level, especially in areas where there is a high incidence of homeless children and young people. These include intermediate treatment centres, information/advice centres, child guidance and assessment services.

5  An educational programme based on the theme 'learning about the process of leaving home' should be developed in youth centres, in schools and other educational establishments and An Chomhairle le Leas Óige could play a major part in developing that programme.

## ADMINISTRATION OF SERVICES

1  The children's services should be provided for by special sections within the Department of Health which should have its own budget and which would not be competing with medical services or large hospitals for scarce resources.

2  The statutory children's services should be fully responsible for all young people under eighteen years of age who cannot stay in their own homes.

3  The statutory children's services should also be responsible for supportive and preventative services to families who are in difficulties or at risk.

4  Hostels should be used only as emergency or short-term accommodation and should be funded in the same manner as other residential homes. Young people out-of-home should not be labelled 'homeless'.

5  All family services should be co-ordinated in each area through child-care boards made up of statutory and voluntary bodies involved. These boards should be responsible for the policy, planning and overview of services in the area. They should operate within a framework with sufficient flexibility, to be adapted to meet the existing needs of children, young people and families in the area.

## RESEARCH

1  The needs of children and young people and the services provided for them need to be constantly monitored, documented and reviewed.

2  Serious research is needed here in Ireland and outside of it, particularly in relation to the following:

- life style activities and needs of children out-of-home

- nature and extent of deficiencies in emergency, short-term and long-term residential provisions and services for young people out-of-home

- alternative education for children and young people out-of-home

- nature and extent of deficiencies in community based services for young people out-of-home

- how to develop appropriate community and youth projects for children out-of-home

- practical action oriented studies and assessments of what directly affects and what can improve the daily lives of children and young people out-of-home

# Appendix

## Statistics on People Contacted by Focus-Point Outreach Team

Number of people contacted by outreach
service, September 1985-February 1986
. . . . . . . . . . . . . . . . . . Total 257*

| *Sex*: | Female | 56 |
| | Male | 201 |

| *Age*: | under 14 | |
| | 14 – 16 | 19 |
| | 16 – 18 | 54 |
| | 18 – 25 | 107 |
| | Over 25 | 77 |

| *Origin*: | Dublin | 201 |
| | Outside Dublin | 45 |
| | Abroad | 11 |

*Accommodation on first contact*:

| Hostel | 55 |
| Squatting/sleeping rough | 65 |
| Dossing | 49 |
| Flat (private/Corporation) | 36 |
| Home (parental) | 29 |
| Hospital | 10 |
| In care | 4 |
| B & B | 2 |
| Unknown | 7 |

*Relationships with these young people varied
in duration. Only young people who fell into
recognisable groups and with whom contact was
maintained over some time are dealt with here.

### GROUP 1 YOUNG WOMEN OUT-OF-HOME

| *Membership*: | | 4 |
| *Age*: | 16 years | 2 |
| | 17 years | 2 |

*Accommodation on first contact*:
| Dossing/sleeping rough | 4 |

### GROUP 2 YOUNG WOMEN OUT-OF-HOME

| *Membership*: | | 8 |
| *Age*: | 14 – 16 | 2 |
| | 16 – 18 | 1 |
| | 18 – 20 | 3 |
| | 20 – 25 | 2 |

*Accommodation on first contact*:
| Squatting/sleeping rough | 4 |
| Flats/sleeping rough | 4 |

### GROUP 3 BOYS ON THEIR OWN

| *Membership*: | | 11 |
| *Age*: | under 14 | 4 |
| | 14 – 16 | 5 |
| | 16 – 18 | 2 |

*Accommodation on first contact*:
| Dossing with well-wishers |
| sleeping rough | 11 |

## GROUP 4 PUNKS

| Membership: | | 14 |
|---|---|---|
| *Age*: | 14 – 16 | 3 |
| | 16 – 18 | 2 |
| | 18 – 20 | 6 |
| | 20 – 25 | 3 |
| *Sex*: | Female | 2 |
| | Male | 12 |

*Accommodation on first contact*:

| | |
|---|---|
| Squatting | 6 |
| Home/dossing | 3 |
| Flats | 1 |
| Home | 4 |

## GROUP 5 DRIFTERS

| Membership: | | 20 |
|---|---|---|
| *Age*: | 14 – 16 | 3 |
| | 16 – 18 | 3 |
| | 18 – 20 | 8 |
| | over 20 | 6 |
| *Sex*: | Female | 5 |
| | Male | 15 |

*Accommodation on first contact*:

| | |
|---|---|
| Sleeping rough/dossing/ squatting | 17 |
| Home | 3 |

## GROUP 6 OLDER MEN'S DRINKING GROUP

| Membership: | | 40 |
|---|---|---|
| *Age*: | 18 – 30 | 26 |
| | under 18 | 14 |
| *Sex*: | Female | — |
| | Male | 40 |

*Accommodation on first contact*:

| | |
|---|---|
| Hostel | 10 |
| Flats/dossing | 21 |
| Squatting | 9 |

## GROUP 7 YOUNG TRAVELLERS

| Membership: | | 19 |
|---|---|---|
| *Age*: | under 14 | 2 |
| | 14 – 16 | 11 |
| | 16 – 18 | 4 |
| | 18 – 20 | 2 |
| *Sex*: | Female | 7 |
| | Male | 12 |

*Accommodation on first contact*:

| | |
|---|---|
| Sleeping rough | 9 |
| Dossing | 2 |
| Hostel | 1 |
| Home | 7 |

# Postscript

'Streetwise' was established in April 1987, as a direct outcome of the Streetwise seminar held in Dublin in March 1987 and while this book was being prepared for press. Already the group includes representation of over twenty-five organisations throughout Ireland and its basic concern is to pursue reforms of policies and services as identified during the seminar.

**Participants in Streetwise seminar**

**Amiens Street, Child Care Centre** David Little, Elizabeth Donohoe
**Arran Quay Resource Centre** Nuala O'Hanlon
**Association of Child Care Workers** May Lynham
**Dr Barnardo's** Christy Kealy, Miriam Mooney, Andrew Logue
**Blaithín** Fran Hayes
**Bray Refuge** Liz McManus, Bernadette Sheerin
**Brú Chaomhín Hostel** Una McCourtney
**Catholic Social Services Conference** Rev William Farrell
**Catholic Youth Council** Brian Murtagh, Tony Foley
**C.C. Communications** Paul Skinneder, John Brady
**Centre Care** John Brophy, Catherine Prendergast
**Centre for Faith and Justice** Pat Davis, Ray Byrne, Geraldine Doherty, Nuala Drake, Patrick Dewis, Peter McVerry
**Charity, Daughters of, Seton House** Judith Connaire, Bernadette Fenessy, Clare Gibbons
**Charity, Daughters of, Sacred Heart Home** Marian Gribbon, Goretti Butler, Jennifer Kidd, Theresa O'Rourke
**Charity, Sisters of, Harolds Cross** Joseph Helen
**Charity, Sisters of, Milltown, Dublin** Marie Molloy, Margaret Gribbon
**Charity, Sisters of, Moore Abbey, Co. Kildare** Mary O'Flaherty, Sheila Ryan
**Charity, Sisters of, Stanhope Street** Margaret Cadden

**Charity, Sisters of, Grianán Training Centre** Carmel Fay, M. Fogarty, Frances Hayes

**Christian Brothers** Liam Murphy

**Coláiste Íosagáin** Máire Ní Mhaolduin

**Comhairle le Leas Óige** Aileen Mulhern, Mary Mooney, Derry O'Connor, Maurice Ahern, Nicholas MacLachlain, Helen Miller, Rita McNulty, Anna Gunning

**Comhlámh** Ciarán Murphy

**Community Action on Drugs** Marian Foster, Mary Johnson

**Concern** Maria Ribeiro

**Contact Magazine, Eastern Health Board** Joe McEvoy

**Council for Social Welfare** Margaret Burns, Pauline Berwick

**Council for the Status of Women** Nora Browne

**Crumlin Youth Support Group** David Farrington, John O'Sullivan

**Department of Health** A. McCabe, A. Alyward, Joe Robins

**Derralossy House, Wicklow** Teresa Healy, Petra Mulvany, Dave Schwartz, Eamon Fitzgerald, Caoimhín Woods

**Donnybrook Youth Club** Sean Humphries, Ann Murphy

**Dublin Committee for Travellers** B. O'Flanagan

**Dublin County Council** Cllr Anne Brady, Cllr Breda Cass, Cllr Anne Elliot, Cllr Ethna Fitzgerald, Cllr Tony Fox, Cllr Martin Lynch, Cllr Bernie Molone, Cllr Teresa Ridge, Cllr Don Tipping, Cllr Michael Gannon, Cllr Eamon Gilmore

**Dublin Institute of Adult Education** Carol McCabe

**Dún Laoire Drugs Awareness Group** Rosie Smith

**Dún Laoire Youth Service** Eithne Gilligan, Michael Kelly, Peter O'Brian, Colette O'Rafferty

**Eastern Health Board** Dymphna Clune

**Eastern Health Board Homeless Persons Unit** Gerry Kenny

**Eastern Health Board Public Health Nurse** Catherine Lanigan

**Eastern Health Board Social Work Services** Olga Estridge, Shane Sheridan, Peggie Walsh, Carmel Murphy, Bernard Morrin

**Eastern Health Board Travellers Unit** Patrick Doogue

**Education Research Centre, St Patrick's College, Dublin** Catherine Lanigan

**European Foundation for the Development of Living and Working Conditions** Wendy O'Conghaile

**Exchange House** Elaine Geiran, John Glynn, Betty Neville, Thomas McDonagh, Donna O'Rourke, Maura Kearney, Catherine Gill, Gordon Fozzard, Victor Foley, John O'Brien, Adrian Eastwood, Pascal Scallon

**Focus-Point** Sarah Moore, Chris Mulvey, Noreen Riordan, Stanislaus Kennedy, Therese Cronin, Leonie Masterson, Angela Brady, Jean Quinn, Grainne Hilton, Siobhan Gibbons, Justin O'Brien, Patricia Donohue, Sile Wall, Olga Cox, Morna Pugh, Majella Mulkeen, Julie Hickey, Dorothy

Carr, Rachel Collier, Michele Ryan, Sharon Farrell, Siobhan Steadman, Karen Fitzsimons, Sandra Mangan, Michele Loftus, Christine O'Donnell, Paula Markey, Rose Mary Cullen, Carrie Lynch, Patricia Murphy, Rita Ryan, Anna Deneher, Kathleen Keegan, Julie Croghan, Conor Butler, Mary Kearney, Olive Mooney, Carol McCabe.

**Foróige** Rita Grant

**Girls' Club** Deirdre Flynn

**Grianán, Dublin** Carmel Fay, Margaret Fogarty

**Grosvenor House** Eileen Ryan

**Hesed Community, Dublin** Mary Maguire, Peter Maguire, Mary Cooney, Ciaran Hurley, G. Hurley

**Holy Faith Sisters, Finglas** Ursula French

**Interaid** Sally MacFarland

**International Alliance of Women** Hilda Trudy

**Institute of Guidance Counsellors** Brid Coyle

**Irish Catholic Magazine** Mary Dundon

**Irish Foundation for Human Development** Tom Ronane

**Irish Red Cross Society** Ann Gallagher

**ISPCC** Cian Ó Tighearnaigh, Tríona Nic Giolla Choille

**Juvenile Liaison Officers** John O'Leary, John Tuohy

**Lakelands Children's Home** Joan Cassidy

**Madonna House, Children's Home** Gerard Bolgar

**Mater Dei Counselling Centre** Claire Hoban, Anne Mallon

**Mater Hospital Child Guidance Clinic** Eugene Donohue

**Mental Health Association of Ireland** Brian Glanville, Mary J. O'Mahony, Finola Colgan

**Mercy, Sisters of, Limerick** Aine Mulholland

**Mincéir Misli** Margaret Maughan, Eileen O'Reilly, Con Carroll, Richard McCann

**Miss Carr's Children's Home** Jennifer Kid, Theresa O'Rourke

**Mrs Smyly's Children's Home** Geraldine Nugent

**National Federation of Youth Clubs** Elizabeth Donohue, May Purcell

**Ógra, Dún Laoghaire** Laura Brosie

**One World** Denis Bergin, Alice Griffin

**PACE** Willie Lawrence, Colman Rutherford

**Peace Corps, Rialto** Crona Gallagher

**Percy Place Hostel** Paul Flynn, John Leinster, Bernadette Egar, Fiona Pryle, Tony Sandford, Mary Kearney, Dave Malone, Con Dowling

**Presentation College, Bray** Geoffrey O'Brian, Daragh O'Kane

**Pro Cathedral** Liam Ó Cuív

**St Anne's Residence** Francis Robinson

**St Anne's School, Milltown** Angela Fahy

**St Claire's, Rathgar** Patricia Wildy, Josephine Laffan

**St David's Youth Club** Eamon Bryan

**St Michael's Assessment Centre, Finglas** Colin Madigan

**St Michael's Youth Project, Inchicore** Terry Webster, Joseph Kennedy, Brian Healy

**St Patrick's College, Maynooth** Emer Nic Reamoinn, Catherine Radge, Scott Boldt, Paul Kelly, Sean Henessey

**St Vincent's Children's Home, Drogheda** Anne Harahan

**Salesian House, Maynooth** Joe Lucey

**Salvation Army** Lt Biddle, Caroline Gleeson, Alice Hill

**Sherrard House Hostel** Eugene McCarthy, Bernadette Bryant, Maura Cullen

**Simon Community, Cork** Patrick Bergin

**Simon Community, Dublin** Phil Flanagan

**Simon Community, Galway** Myles Murphy, Bill Hawkins, Larry Conlett, Dave Warner, Agnes Hill

**Social Service Centre, St Catherine's, Carlow** Mary Kenny

**South Eastern Health Board** Sr Marie McGuinness, Helen O'Brien, Margaret O'Meara, Mary Sheedy

**South Inner City Community Development Association** Nel Carney, Geraldine Regan

**SUSS Centre, Ballymun** Cathleen Maher, Bernard Cummins, Yvonne Weir

**Team Educational Theatre** Jim Nolan

**Trinity College, Dublin** Gerry Whyte, Robbie Gilligan

**Trudder House, Newtownmountkennedy, Co. Wicklow** Donal Burke, Patricia Dowling, Noel Geary, Irene McKeowin, Petra Mulvey

**UNICEF** Maurice Harmon, Dorothy Archer, Ena Byrne, Donna Lyttle

**University College, Cork** Anne Doyle

**University College, Dublin — Staff, Social Science Dept.** Mary Horkan

**Western Way Day Centre, Dublin** Brian McMillan, J. Keirns

**YMCA, Cork** John Bausany

**Youth Action Project, Ballymun** Mary Ellen McCann, Geraldine O'Donovan, Queenie Barnes

**Youth Centre, St Saviour's** Eamon Bryan, Julie Keirnes

**Youth Club, Donnybrook** Sean Humphreys, Anne Murphy

**Youth Committee, Waterford** Joe Hennebry, Joe Gough

**Youth Development Project Ógra Dun Dealgan** Declan Brassil, Laura Brossie

**Youth Encounter Project, Clonmel** Colm Gregory, James Golesberry, Paul Hogan, Peter Kieran

**Youth Service, Blanchardstown** Jacinta Conroy

**Youth Services, Galway** Joe Carmody, Noel Daly, Marie Dunane, Marie Donohoe, Laura Fahy, Rosemary Kearns, Pearl O'Kennedy, Joe Conroy, Larry Conlett

**Youth Service, VEC Tallaght** John Cahill, Fiona O'Grady

**Individuals**
Una Blake, Charlie Moloney, Louise Lowe, Maura Kearney, Paul O'Callaghan, Sean Houlihan, Fergus Comerford, Terry Ford, Des Finnegan, Charlie Mulrooney, Edward Garrigan, Charlie Mularnay, Joseph Doyle, Paul O'Callaghan, Eileen Ryan, Br Liam Murphy, Sr Marie McEvoy, Brona Kavanagh, Tony Cleary, Rita Gannon, Joseph Feedy, Eugene McCarthy, Joy Rudd, Sr Thomas Redmond, Sr Mary O'Connell